HOLIDAY CRUISING ON INLAND WATERWAYS

'Master Mariner' 41 ft narrow beam cruiser, on the Grand Union near Marsworth. The cruiser was built by John Fisher of Peppersworth Ltd

HOLIDAY CRUISING ON INLAND WATERWAYS

CHARLES HADFIELD
and
MICHAEL STREAT

with plates, text illustrations, and Stanford's
Inland Cruising Map of England for Larger Craft

DAVID & CHARLES : NEWTON ABBOT

ISBN 0 7153 5109 5

First published 1968
Second edition 1971

Printed in Great Britain
by Latimer Trend & Company Limited Plymouth
for David & Charles (Publishers) Limited
Newton Abbot Devon

Contents

List of Illustrations

9

List of Illustrations

TEXT ILLUSTRATIONS

MAP

Stanford's *Inland Cruising Map for Larger Craft*

Preface

Britain's inland waterways are becoming better known each year, and the 1967 White Paper announcing that a cruising network would be authorised has greatly increased interest in them; yet many hesitate to try a boating holiday because they don't know how to work a lock, or think they might lose their way on the canals.

So into this book we have tried to put what the intending holiday-maker and, we hope, the later potential boat-owner will find interesting and useful to know. It is roughly divided into four sections: Chapters 1 and 2 are general background to the inland waterways system and can be postponed if you want to get on; 3, 4 and 5 are about actual cruising; 6, 7, 8 and 9 about hiring, buying, converting and maintaining boats; while Chapter 10 brings together miscellaneous information you may find useful.

We have found collaboration easy and pleasant, but because Chapter 1 can only be a personal statement, one of us has written it. For the rest of the book we are both responsible. May it help others to the pleasures we ourselves have known for so long.

CHARLES HADFIELD
MICHAEL STREAT

11

CHAPTER ONE

The Pleasures of Boating

It was eighteen years ago, when few motor-boats were about, that I first took out a cruiser on the canals. My children were enchanted by the checked curtains in the windows of the forward cabin where they were to sleep; my wife approved of the galley and ticked off the groceries we had ordered from our hirer; and I discarded my city suit for flannels and a roll-neck sweater, for it was April.

We started from Stone in Staffordshire on the Trent & Mersey Canal, climbing the locks towards Stoke-on-Trent. There was one bad moment when my visual memory showed me a paddle-bar not fully down on the lower gate of a lock below the one I had just left. There followed a successful struggle of conscience with laziness, and I walked back, in time to see the pound below my lock running itself dry. Hoping no lock-keeper would arrive, I hurriedly shut the paddle, ran back to the lock above, opened everything and restored the situation. Ever since, I have trained myself, as I leave a lock, to glance back at the paddle-bars. Are they all down—right down?

We moored that night above Etruria top-lock in the middle of the Five Towns. Not, you will say, a picturesque spot. Maybe not, but there one can look over the valley to works where every so often a bright glare lights the sky as furnaces are tapped; and just along the towpath, beside the canal, Josiah Wedgwood's original eighteenth-century pottery building stands; and down a side street is the pub where an old, old gentleman told me that Stoke-on-Trent was the healthiest place in England—and he ought to have known, for he had never been out of it.

Next day we went through Harecastle tunnel. There are some, like my wife and daughter, who say that Harecastle is narrow and low and dark. Send them below to the cabin to play halma, but stay on deck yourself, and see how successfully you can keep a 7 ft boat in

13

the centre of a 9 ft waterway. Before you've learned the trick, you are out again, at the Blue Bell at Kidsgrove.

Then we went up the Macclesfield Canal. All the way up we bought bottles of beer, marking each with the pub of origin—starting with the Blue Bell—and all the way back we returned the empties and had one on the threepences. The Macclesfield to us means mooring at Marple, and, as darkness falls, watching the lights come out on the hills all round as the towns transform themselves to glow-worm embroidery worked on the Pennine slopes.

And so down the Trent & Mersey to Middlewich, turn left for Barbridge, left again for the Shropshire Union; a first meeting with Sam Lomas of Autherley lock (dear Sam, now dead, who loved canals and remembered so much of their past); up Wolverhampton twenty-one locks in 1 hour 55 minutes, I say it with pride; along the Birmingham main line to spend the night in the peace of the basin at Worcester Bar, a stone's throw from the city's centre; then down Farmer's Bridge locks to the Birmingham & Fazeley Canal; left for the Coventry; a pause, as all good boaters pause, at the *Swan* at Fradley; and so back to Stone, in two weeks of canalling. I've done many cruises since, but details of that first run are as clear in my mind today as eighteen years ago, and I have felt few pleasures more keenly.

Who can define or explain the enjoyment of a boat on water, on the Broads, a river, or a canal? Of course it's not idyllic. Sometimes it rains. Things can go wrong with the boat (one night I had to balance a pudding basin on my stomach to catch the drips through the cabin roof). Things can get wrapped round the propeller. But there are all the times when it doesn't rain, the early mornings when the mist lies over the land and the wind ripples the water ahead, and through a bridge-hole one can see the uptilted beams of a lock. The smell of coffee and frying bacon; waving to passengers in a parallel train; rides given to children from a passing car, returned to their bewildered parents at the next bridge; lying on deck and lazily watching the trees' shadows; having time to look at flowers and plants, birds and animals; and at night returning from a walk along the towpath to see the cabin lights shining on the water.

Some like to keep their boats moving, to explore new waterways and revisit old pleasures; others are weekenders, who base their craft on a permanent mooring, and take it out for a potter round: some indeed seldom leave the bank, so happily are they engaged in scraping and polishing and painting and splicing and gossiping. But what

14

does it matter, so long as you are happy, and are not a nuisance to your neighbour?

Perhaps because of this enjoyment, motor-boating on inland waterways is becoming more and more popular. It's slow, and it's relaxing. After a fortnight's cruising at 3 mph, I defy anyone to be tense. It's safe. Accidents are rare, and when they occur, are usually the result of neglecting the most obvious precautions. It's popular with children, who find endless things to do on the boat and ashore; and it suits all tastes. If you are gregarious, you can join a boat club and a society or two, and spend your time with like-minded people. If you are a nature-lover, you will find a wealth of wild life along the inland waterways, the flowers and grasses of the canals, the birds and animals of the Broads. If you are a solitary, you can be as quiet and as alone as you like.

This book is, therefore, an invitation to the water. If the idea is new to you, then maybe you would be wise to start by hiring a cruiser for a week or two, to see how you like it. If you do, hire once more, and meanwhile study maps, read a few books, do some planning, and then buy a boat of your own. We have tried to tell you what you may need to know and certainly enough to get you started. But in the end each boat is an island inhabited only by you and those you choose to invite. On it you are king, with over 2,000 miles of waterways ahead of you. What are your orders? To Oxford or Cambridge, York, Newark, Lincoln or Worcester? Skipton, Shardlow or Stoke Bruerne? Cowroast or Sutton's Stop? Let's go.

CHAPTER TWO

The Inland Waterways Today

Even before man learned to build a boat, he floated logs down rivers. With a boat, he had the means of transporting both people and goods.

In our own country, the Romans used the principal rivers, and also built canals for drainage and transport: the Fossdyke, used by barges and motor cruisers today, and the Caerdyke. From early medieval times the great rivers—Thames, Severn, Trent and others—were increasingly used for transport in days when roads were useless for heavy goods. This was also the case in eastern England, where almost until our own century the Fenland waterways and the Broads were the main means of moving goods, and to some extent people, about.

Most British canals were built between 1760 and 1840. Some extended a river navigation further upwards, or by-passed difficult stretches. Others connected two rivers together by passing over or through the high ground that divided them. Others had no connexion with rivers, and ran from collieries or mines to a town that used the raw materials, and others were branches off bigger canals, serving towns or works away from the main lines.

All these built up into an interconnected network, over which individuals, or partnerships, but very seldom canal companies, worked their carrying craft. But because they were built each by its own private company, and usually for local purposes, these canals were constructed with different widths, depths and lock sizes, as cash and water supplies permitted.

When, in the 1840s, railways began to compete seriously with waterways, they had several advantages; they carried their own goods; they could cut coal and merchandise rates against the canals, and recoup themselves from passenger revenue; they were faster; and they soon built up a bigger network. Some waterway companies modernised themselves and fought back; others sold out; others went

16

1 (*Above*) Inland cruising is fun for all the family: simple meals in the open air taste better than the finest restaurant fare; (*below*) not quite Bristol fashion, but nobody minds. A hire cruiser in a lock on the upper Thames. Note the flower garden.

2 (*Above*) Typical Broadland scene with a big motor hire cruiser passing one of the many delightful waterside summer houses; (*below*) peaceful moorings on the Oxford Canal: two hire cruisers moor together beneath weeping willows a mile or so from the city centre.

bankrupt. Then came the motor lorry, able to pick up goods at point of origin and carry them direct to destination, which competed against both canals and railways. More waterways now went out of use.

So, at the end of the war in 1945, we had in Britain a number of big waterways, mainly canalised rivers, carrying large tonnages of goods, and a selection of small canals and rivers upon which barges and narrow boats were still struggling, with diminishing hope of success, to compete with lorry and railway.

THE BEGINNINGS OF MOTOR-BOATING

Then came pleasure boating. Pioneers had explored the canals before, in skiffs or canoes; like E. Temple Thurston in *The Flower of Gloster*, by horse-drawn barge; or in motor-boats, like George Westall, who worked round most of them, and published *Inland Cruising* in 1908, an ancestor of the book you are reading now. Austin Neal had come down the Oxford Canal, was at Braunston when he heard that the first Great War had been declared, and found it difficult to get petrol: 'The Government are taking it all, sir; I expect they want it for the airmen.' In spite of the war, however, he called his book *Canals, Cruises and Contentment*. Bonthron also published *My Holidays on Inland Waterways*, another cruising guide to 2,000 miles of water. It sold well, but, all the same, only a very few went motor-boating on canals before 1945.

NARROW BOAT AND THE INLAND WATERWAYS ASSOCIATION

In 1944 L. T. C. Rolt first published *Narrow Boat*, still in print, a narrative of a cruise in a converted craft. Beautifully written, it was exactly to the taste of a public long deprived of such pleasures, and opened up new possibilities of enjoyment as soon as the war should be over. In the same year Charles Hadfield, one of the authors of this book, published a smaller book, *English Rivers and Canals*, which also caught the public mood. The Inland Waterways Association was founded as a direct consequence of *Narrow Boat*, with Robert Aickman as chairman and Rolt as secretary. As far back as 1935 a cruiser hiring firm, the Inland Cruising Association, had been founded at Christleton near Chester by G. F. Wain and others; it had thirteen boats by 1939. This firm, now called Inland Hire Cruisers Ltd, is carried on by Mr David B. Wain. After the war R. H. Wyatt set up a hiring business at Stone, soon to be followed by others, among them Michael Streat, the other author of this book. Slowly motor-boating on canals increased, encouraged by the national demand for the quiet countryside pleasures it offers, but held back by uncertainty over the future of many canals.

THE BRITISH WATERWAYS BOARD

In December 1962 the British Waterways Board took over the control of most navigable rivers and canals from the British Transport Commission. It was now possible to plan a future for the smaller waterways on their use for pleasure, and not for transport. As this future became more secure, so the number of boats placed on the waterways quickly increased, and revenue from them grew. In 1966, in a White Paper, the Government for the first time accepted pleasure cruising as a reason for keeping canals open, and in 1967 announced that a cruising network would be authorised and financed; the difficult transition had been made.

So, today, we have a number of big waterways, Trent, Severn, Aire & Calder, Weaver and others, which are maintained for transport, but which pleasure craft can use; and a network of smaller canals and rivers upon which a few small commercial craft still operate, but whose future lies with the pleasure boat.

Outside the network which passed at nationalisation in 1947 to the British Transport Commission, and thence to the British Waterways Board, were some waterways upon which motor-boating had developed earlier, like the Thames and the Broads, and others upon which it is now steadily spreading, notably the Fenland waterways based on the Great Ouse.

Boat hiring firms, those with boat-building and repair yards, or those offering berthing facilities, have established themselves on all these, and, shops, restaurants, pubs and garages have begun to realise that motor-boating people have needs to be satisfied. The expansion of motor-boating is therefore bringing its own responses. One is the growth of boat clubs; another the increasing interest taken in schemes to improve canal amenities, especially in town areas, so that urban cruising may be made more attractive. The biggest plan is for the development of the Lea Valley, but in London, Birmingham, Stoke-on-Trent and elsewhere, local civic efforts are being put to waterway

20

improvement. Another is the interest taken in waterway restoration, in ensuring that the country's system of attractive pleasure cruising waterways, whether urban or rural, shall be not only maintained but increased. The Lower Avon, the lower Stratford-upon-Avon Canal, the Stourbridge Canal, Linton Lock, the Great Ouse locks near Bedford, have been restored, and work is going on now on the Kennet & Avon Canal, the Caldon branch, and the Upper Avon below Stratford. Again, on the Broads and the Fenland rivers, a number of old channels have been dredged and made usable, and efforts are all the time being made to extend the cruising grounds.

Those who cruise these waterways do so for pleasure; for the quiet water, the reflection of the trees in the Broads river, the sight of a heron flapping away, the sound of water running through lock gates, a canal-side pub's open fire on a chilly evening, the thrill of passing over a great aqueduct. Yet, if one looks with an interested eye, there is so much more to see.

COMMERCIAL CRAFT

Except for the coasters or the occasional tug and barges that go from Yarmouth up the Yare to Norwich, these have gone from the Broads, though perhaps you will see *Albion*, the last of the black-hulled sailing wherries, now owned by a trust and sailed from time to time.

On the smaller canals there are still narrow boats, 70 ft × 7 ft, a motor towing a butty. Each has a cabin, warmed by a coal range, and traditionally decorated with wall painting, lace-edged plates, and plenty of brasswork. The doors, and perhaps the cabin sides, will be painted with castle scenes and patterns of roses. A pair of these craft carry about 50 tons, and may be crewed by a husband and wife, or by two men.

On big commercial waterways like the Aire & Calder (from Goole to Leeds and Wakefield), or the Sheffield & South Yorkshire (near Goole to Doncaster and Sheffield) you can pass what at first seems to be a water-snake: a tug at the head, then a wooden boat's bow, followed by nineteen almost square iron tanks all lashed together and laden with coal. The false bow breaks the water, and behind it you will notice that tightened chains have pulled the first two craft a little upwards to enable the water to slide more easily underneath. These tanks, locally called pans or 'Tom Puddings' were built in the 60s of the last century to be pushed by a tug in groups of six; then the tug was put in front and locks lengthened for the present trains, each carrying some 700 tons and passing locks in one operation.

At Goole each pan is hoisted and tipped into a ship's hold. To carry coal to the new Ferrybridge 'C' power station at Knottingley, 540-ton barges built in three 180-ton sections, and powered by a tug, are used. Each section is hoisted and tipped.

On these waterways you will see John Harker's big tankers; there will also be large self-propelled barges going perhaps to Leeds; smaller 'Sheffield' type barges (those about 60 ft × 15 ft, which can use the locks above Doncaster), and still smaller 'Westcountry' barges. These are about 56 ft × 14 ft, and can use the Leeds & Liverpool or Calder & Hebble locks; by the former they can still reach the Westcountry (Lancashire); by the latter they once could, until the Rochdale Canal closed.

LOCKS

Narrow boats on the one hand, these big craft on the other, define the principal distinction to be made about waterways, the size of the locks—except on the Broads, where there are none. Narrow canals, predominant in the Midlands, were built with locks about 7 ft wide to take narrow boats; therefore only motor-boats up to this beam can use them. Broad waterways, which include all the principal rivers and many canals branching from them, have locks at least 14 ft wide, though on the Grand Union the ruling bridge width on the upper part to Birmingham is 13 ft 3 in, in spite of the lock widths. Stanford's map in this book will show you which are narrow canals.

Most locks are singletons, though some are grouped in flights (a flight is a series of locks each one of which is 400 yards or less from the next) to overcome a steep rise in the ground. The biggest flight in the country is that of 30 narrow locks at Tardebigge on the Worcester & Birmingham Canal; others are Devizes on the Kennet & Avon (29 broad, not now usable), Wolverhampton on the Birmingham Canal Navigations (21 narrow), Wigan on the Leeds & Liverpool (22 broad), and Hatton on the Grand Union Canal (21 broad). When the ground rose very steeply, the canal engineer built locks in staircases: that is, the top gate of a lower lock is also the bottom gate of the one above it. These often occur in pairs or threes, but there are two staircases of five narrow locks each at Foxton on the Leicester line, one of five broad locks at Bingley on the Leeds & Liverpool, and one of eight big locks at Banavie on the Caledonian Canal. Abroad there are fine staircases at Béziers on the Canal du Midi in France, on the Göta Canal in Sweden and the Bandak and Halden Canals in Norway.

Again, most locks have ordinary mitre gates that open and close like a door. Occasionally, as on the rivers Nene and Great Ouse, one of the gates is made to rise vertically. These guillotine gates make flood control easier.

LIFTS

An alternative to locks is a lift, when boats are floated into a tank to be raised vertically to the upper level. There used to be several in Britain, but the only one now used is at Anderton; this transfers boats between the Trent & Mersey Canal above and the Weaver River below. Opened in 1875, it has two caissons or tanks each 75 ft × 15 ft 6 in × 5 ft, and a vertical rise of 50 ft 4 in. Originally it was worked hydraulically, but it is now electrically operated. No one should miss a ride in it. There are others in Belgium, Germany and Canada.

Another way of getting boats from one level to another was by wheeled tanks running on a sloping ramp—called an inclined plane. The ruins of one of these can be seen near Foxton locks, on the Leicester line. A huge new one has been built at Ronquières in Belgium, and a rather smaller one at Arzviller in France.

TUNNELS

So long as you have a good light forward, there is no need to be nervous about tunnels. Indeed the mellow brickwork's shapes and colours, streaks of many coloured water, occasional ventilation shafts, distance markings, and the hope of passing another boat, give one plenty to look at. The longest now in regular use is Blisworth on the Grand Union (3,056 yd or about 1¾ miles); this is a broad tunnel in which 7 ft craft can pass. So is Braunston (2,042 yd) on the same canal (with a slight 'S' bend in it), and Netherton (3,027 yd) between the Birmingham Canal main line and the Dudley Canal on the way to the Stourbridge. Harecastle (2,926 yd) on the Trent & Mersey is a narrow tunnel, with a rather low roof in places. Having no shafts, it is ventilated by fans at the southern end, and therefore doors across this portal are kept shut until your boat is approaching them.

Dudley narrow tunnel can be investigated from the Birmingham end, though you have (for the time being) to turn at the far end and come back. Get in touch with someone from the Dudley Canal Trust (see p 139) if you want to go through. It is a remarkable experience. Other longish tunnels you can cruise through, all of them broad, are West Hill (or Wast Hill), Worcester & Birmingham Canal, 2,726 yd; Foulridge, Leeds & Liverpool Canal, 1,640 yd; Crick, Leicester line, 1,528 yd; Preston Brook, Trent & Mersey Canal, 1,239 yd; Husbands Bosworth, Leicester line, 1,166 yd; Islington, Regent's Canal, 960 yd; and Saddington, Leicester line, 880 yd. The longest ever built in Britain was Standedge (narrow) under the Pennines (5,698 yd), but this is not accessible.

AQUEDUCTS

These are perhaps the most spectacular of canal engineering works. A cruise up the Llangollen Canal would be worth while if only to cross the Dee Valley on the 19-arched iron trough Pontcysyllte aqueduct opened in 1805, 1,007 ft long, 121 ft above the Dee at its highest point. On your way you will also cross Chirk aqueduct, which takes the canal on ten arches over the river Ceiriog. You can also take your cruiser over the unique Barton swing aqueduct, which carries the Bridgewater Canal over the Manchester Ship Canal. It is 235 ft long, weighs 1,450 tons, and can be swung sideways out of the way of ships. Other interesting ones to pass over are Rennie's 5-arched masonry aqueduct that takes the Lancaster Canal over the river Lune; the Victorian iron tied-arch aqueduct that carries the Aire & Calder Navigation over the river Calder at Stanley Ferry below Wakefield; Wolverton iron trough over the Great Ouse on the Grand Union, and the single-arched Dane aqueduct just below Bosley locks on the Macclesfield Canal. There are many others, reducing in size until they become culverts. An oddity is at Brinklow on the Oxford Canal. Originally a 12-arched aqueduct (houses were to have been built inside some of the land arches), it was later converted to an embankment, but on one side the old arches can still be seen.

BRIDGES

Canal bridges are an enduring delight. The design varies with the engineer who built them, and occasionally with the landowner who demanded something special. Almost every bend in a canal brings one in sight of brick or masonry, enclosing a silver pattern of water and trees. Scattered among the fixed bridges are those that swing or lift or roll. Constructed for the accommodation of farmers whose land had been divided by the canal, usually of wood, such a bridge is sometimes an annoyance to a boater in a hurry, who has to leap ashore to swing it to one side, or lift it clear of the waterway. But, as the sun sets, and a last bird skims the length of the canal, the image of a lift bridge's splendid structure, perhaps on the Llangollen Canal, or the railed curve of one on the Oxford Canal, sticks in the mind long after the cruise has ended.

There are memorable bridges of other kinds also: the new motor-way bridges, or railway bridges with lifting spans, like those on the Trent or the Aire & Calder, or with a swinging section, as on the dis-mantled Severn bridge over the Gloucester & Sharpness Canal; and, at the opposite extreme, the eye-of-a-needle bridges—Fotheringhay on the Nene, Newark on the Trent, the Glory Hole at Lincoln, Eckington on the Lower Avon, or that over the Great Ouse at St Ives which has a chantry chapel in the centre.

TOWPATHS

A word here about towpaths, or haling ways, as they are called in East Anglia. Originally, of course, they were built for towing-horses. Now they enable you and me to get quickly to and from our boats, and others to fish or stroll beside the water. They are not usually rights of way. Those with business on the waterway use them, but the public only with a walking permit (it costs 12½p a year), or on sufferance.

Towpaths change sides from time to time on canals by a bridge, often designed with curving approaches so that the horses could cross the water without the towing lines being cast off. On rivers they had to be ferried over, and one can often trace the 'rovings' where ferry-boats carried them across, and perhaps identify the old ferrymen's houses.

When a towpath came to a tunnel, it might pass through it beside the canal, as in the Chirk tunnel of the Llangollen Canal. But, more commonly, the boat was legged or shafted through by the crew, while the horses were led along a path over the top. Most of these paths can still be traced, and used by nervous members of one's family who, eccentrically, don't like tunnels—even canal ones.

WATERSIDE PLACES AND BUILDINGS

A number of towns and villages owe their existence to a waterway, having grown up near a terminus or a junction to provide warehouses, wharves, and houses for those whose livelihood lay with the boats. Such as Goole, built by the Aire & Calder Company where the navigation joined the Yorkshire Ouse, Runcorn (Bridgewater Canal and the Mersey), Ellesmere Port (Ellesmere Canal, later the Shropshire Union, and the Mersey, later the Manchester Ship Canal), Stourport (Staffs & Worcs Canal and the Severn) and Shardlow, on the Trent & Mersey Canal just above its junction with the Trent.

At many places on the Broads and Fenland waterways, up and down the navigable rivers, and scattered over the canals, one finds little groups of old buildings that owe their origin to waterborne trade: one or two warehouses, a pub, a group of cottages, a shop. Some are notably picturesque, like Ashleworth on the Severn above Gloucester, with its wharf, warehouse, pub, and shelter for the ferryman whose job it was to carry towing horses across the river, or Fradley, where the Coventry Canal joins the Trent & Mersey. Some are humbly utilitarian, like Kidsgrove at the junction of the Macclesfield Canal with the Trent & Mersey; some just pleasant, like West Stockwith at the junction of the Chesterfield Canal with the Trent.

Then there are the houses—lockhouses, tunnel-keepers' houses, bridge-keepers' houses, each canal having its own characteristic buildings. Unfortunately, these become fewer as the years go by. Where they are still needed for today's reduced manpower, it is often cheaper, and a great deal more comfortable for the staff, to build a new house than to modernise and enlarge the old one. As in so many other fields, it is necessary to balance the charm and attraction of the old against the needs of the present. But many still stand, each a discovery of the working architecture of the time when it was built.

Fortunately, many canalside and riverside pubs remain. Once they supplied working boatmen or ferry passengers; now they have new customers in those who come by motor-boat, or in cars to sit beside the water and watch the boats go by. To take one short stretch of the Grand Union, how pleasant is the *Boat* at Stoke Bruerne, the *Admiral Nelson* and the *Rose & Castle* at Braunston, the *Blue Lias* at Stockton, the *Two Boats* at Long Itchington, or the *Cape of Good Hope* near Warwick! And on the Broads and the Fenland waterways, all of us can remember the pleasures of mooring up and lazing away an evening at some special pub, perhaps *The Locks* at Geldeston lock or the *Fish & Duck* at Pope's Corner. Here, too, at Holywell on the Great Ouse, *The Ferry Boat* claims an existence from 1068.

WATER

We tend to take the water in a canal for granted. It is there because, when each canal began, the Act of Parliament under which it was built gave the company power to take water from rivers and streams near its line. Certain sources of supply, important as water power to millers, or for other reasons, were often specifically excluded.

Some sources could be directly tapped, usually by feeders, open water channels connecting a river or stream with the canal, or by pumping upwards from a river at a lower level or from a well.

Often, however, these did not yield enough, and had to be supplemented by specially-built reservoirs in which water could be impounded and held until it was wanted. These still feed the canal system, being helped when required by water pumped back from lower levels to those higher, to be used again.

A broad lock holds about 60,000 gallons of water; a narrow lock about 25,000. When, therefore, your boat moves down through the lock, this amount of water leaves the upper pound (they call it a basin in the north), that is the stretch of water above the lock up to the next one, and falls into the pound below the lock. If you have had to fill the lock first before going down, then double these quantities will have been used. As your boat moves down the canal, so it takes a lockful of water with it. Therefore it is always necessary to have a good supply of water coming in to the summit level, or topmost pound of the canal, for this cannot gain, only lose, from lockage.

Each pound below the summit gains water at one end and loses water at the other, as the locks are worked. Supplies may also enter the canal from feeders or side streams at any point. Excess water runs round the locks in culverts or open streams—you can find them if you look—or occasionally over the gates themselves. Should there still be too much water, perhaps because of a sudden storm, then run-offs over the canal banks are provided to take the excess into the nearest stream. Normally, canal water is still until the working of a lock creates a slight movement, but some canals do have a current. For instance, so much water for sale to water undertakings is run down the Llangollen Canal from the Dee that the ½ mph current is perceptible, especially under bridges and in tunnels.

On a river navigation water is passing downstream, and there is always a current. The main flow runs over the weirs, placed beside the lock, which merely diverts what is needed for its own operation. River levels cannot be maintained steady like those on canals, and, after heavy rain, a river may rise several feet, until, perhaps, the weirs can hardly be seen, and then run much faster. Under such conditions a point is reached when craft cannot get under the bridges, or cannot make headway against the stream, and have to wait for the river to fall. Most do so as quickly as they have risen.

Tides hardly affect most of the Broads, except for Yarmouth and Breydon Water (find out about these before attempting them) but tide tables and computers are available and tell you high or low water times. On the lower stretches of the big rivers, however, such as the Trent below Cromwell lock, the Severn from Gloucester, and the Yorkshire Ouse from Naburn, the tide is a factor to be reckoned with.

WHO RUNS THE CANALS, AND HOW?

The total staff of the British Waterways Board is just over 3,000. These look after some 2,000 miles of waterway, man the Board's fleet of boats and provide the administration. Scattered as they are up and down the country, few and far between, canal men are self-reliant and independent. If something goes wrong, it is they who have to act. Others will come to their help, but in the meantime they alone have to get stop-planks in to cut off a stretch of canal with a burst culvert, or do whatever else is necessary.

The Board has two regions, Northern based on Leeds, Southern on Gloucester. Here are the regional engineers, responsible to the Board's principal engineer and his assistant at headquarters. Working for them are the seven area engineers, four for the north at Wigan, Castleford, Northwich and Nottingham, and three for the south at Birmingham, Gloucester and London. Under each area engineer are one or more area inspectors, to whom the section inspectors work. Each of these has a section of canal or river—perhaps 20 or 30 miles —under his charge. He is responsible for it, and for the work of the lock-keepers, lengthsmen, and maintenance men who work on it. Water engineers, who have to know a good deal of civil, mechanical, electrical and hydraulic engineering, are responsible for the safety of banks and structures; for piling the banks against erosion, and dredging the channel; for locks, wharves and buildings of all kinds, for the Board's craft and repair depots, and for the care and maintenance of reservoirs.

Over against the engineering side, which keeps the canals ready for use, is the Freight Services Division, which seeks traffic and deals with it. The head of this Division is at headquarters. To him officers work who are responsible for getting traffic for the Board's fleets and for their warehouses and docks. There are also the sales representatives in each area who seek business, the depot (warehouse) and dock managers, and the superintendents in charge of the Board's coal compartment boat and general merchandise fleets. Pleasure cruising matters are the responsibility of Amenity Services Division, while other departments deal with estates, water sales and administration. At the top is a general manager working to the Board itself.

Other navigation authorities have similar though less extensive structures.

These are the waterways, old, but fulfilling modern purposes for trade and pleasure. Those who work on them enjoy them; those who cruise on them return again and again. Let us find out for ourselves what they have to offer.

CHAPTER THREE

Planning a Cruise

The tranquil waterways await the discriminating explorer, and offer true holiday enjoyment in every mile. But where to start? You have three main choices, with several sub-choices. Without question, the most popular holiday cruising area in the country is the Broads—popularly known as 'The Norfolk Broads', but extending through both Norfolk and Suffolk. The Broads offer some 200 miles of safe inland cruising, comprising rivers and wide, reed-fringed lakes that are the 'Broads' themselves. Broadland was the cradle of the holiday hire business in this country and holiday craft have been available on these waters for over 60 years. Broads firms pioneered holiday hiring and have been the pace-setters ever since. More than 2,000 craft are available for hire there, most of them now linked for advertising and booking through three major agencies. These produce full-colour brochures the size of a large magazine, containing photographs, plans and descriptions of all craft available for hire, and much general background information on the pleasures of Broads cruising. In addition to these (see Chapter 10 for addresses), there are smaller agencies and independent firms.

As a holiday cruising area, Broadland has much to commend it. First and foremost, the Broads offer *easy* cruising. The entire system is on one level, with no locks to interrupt movement or intimidate the novice. Although tidal, the effects of ebb and flow are not pronounced except in limited areas (notably at Great Yarmouth where special caution and knowledge *is* required) so that boat handling is in general not complicated by the effects of swift-flowing water. For much of the way, the water's edge is soft, natural bank, usually fringed by reeds, so that running aground as a result of a mistake or mishap is rarely the cause of serious damage. Having been a cruising area for so long, the Broads have an abundance of waterside facilities for the visiting boatman: moorings are readily available everywhere, and provision and other shops, waterside pubs and restaurants abound. The many boatyards along the cruising routes additionally ensure that service, if needed as a result of mishap or mechanical trouble, is quickly and efficiently available. And, of course, the sea and the East Coast resorts of Yarmouth and Lowestoft, and many smaller seaside villages, are all within a short distance.

Broadland scenery is superb, and the weather in East Anglia generally kind, with more sunshine and less rain than any other part of the country. Little wonder that with all these advantages, Broads cruising has become enormously popular today. Indeed, so sought after have such holidays become that many observers feel that in the height of the season there are just too many craft on the move for the available cruising water, and experienced Broads hands, as a result, will often only visit their favourite cruising ground early or late in the year, when the main rush has abated. Others turn away altogether to explore less publicised waters.

Second to the Broads, in terms of amenities for cruising holidays, comes the River Thames. This waterway, like the Broads, has long been popular, with many old-established boatyards offering holiday craft for hire. Cruising on the Thames is not quite so simple as on the Broads, as there are, of course, locks to be passed, 43 in all on the 120 miles of navigable waterway from Lechlade down to the end of the non-tidal river at Teddington. However, all Thames locks are operated by lock-keepers so that, apart from steering his boat in and out of the lock chambers (which will in high summer take some reasonable skill, as the locks are often packed full of boats) the holiday skipper will not have to assume any responsibility for actual lock operation. Thames locks, like the whole course of the river, are all maintained in first-rate working condition by the extremely efficient controlling body, the Thames Conservancy, and many are surrounded by beautiful gardens lovingly laid out and cared for by the lock-keepers. Most holiday skippers, even if they start off with slight feelings of apprehension about locks, soon come to look on locking through as enjoyable punctuation, which provides variety and interest to the daily journey.

Thames waterside amenities for the boatman are numerous and excellent: magnificent hotels and restaurants abound, with lawns sloping down to waterside moorings for visiting craft, so that eating ashore is practicable and pleasant, though often fairly expensive. Shopping is easy and there are enough boatyards (many of them linked via the Thames Hire Cruiser Association) to offer prompt service to any hire craft in trouble.

Although non-tidal above Teddington the Thames is, of course, a flowing river, with a downstream current for which the holiday skipper must always make allowances. Generally, however, this current is not marked in the normal summer season and presents no navigational problems. However, it can become pronounced following long periods of heavy rain, and this can present difficulties in spring and autumn. Very occasionally at these times the level rises to flood conditions and when this happens hire craft are normally not permitted to cruise.

Probably no river in the world has had as many books written about it as the Thames (two of them are listed on p 145) and no other river in this country offers quite the variety and contrasts of countryside. As a river for holiday cruising it is without equal and the boatman who cannot find peace and pleasure along its winding reaches is surely very hard to please.

The third of the main cruising choices is the canal system—or, to be more exact, the canal and river system largely (but not wholly) controlled by the British Waterways Board. Cruising on the canal system differs fundamentally from cruising on the Broads or the Thames. First, the canals and rivers offer for exploration over 2,000 miles of navigable waterway, mostly man-made, covering much of England so that the choice of cruising scenery is almost unlimited. Second, these do *not* offer the highly developed holiday amenities of the Broads and the Thames. Waterside hotels and restaurants, dance halls and holiday provision shops, all aimed at securing trade from the boating holiday-maker, hardly exist. Hotels and restaurants there are, of course, but almost all are the small hotels and restaurants of the country towns and villages round, near or through which the canal may happen to run. Waterside pubs exist, but they will be quiet, country pubs originally built for the trade of the bygone working boatmen, often with empty stables behind them in which the boat horses were bedded down for the night. You'll be welcome in them all, but it will be the reserved welcome of the countryside, not the seasonal glad-hand of the sophisticated holiday pub.

Again, cruising the canals is harder work than cruising on the Broads or Thames. There are many locks, and none of them (or almost none) is manned. You must work them yourself. As you heave on the balance beams of the lock gates to open them you may notice that your hands are pulling at oak worn smooth by the hands of generations of boatmen before you. The canals are still, with no tides or currents to complicate your cruising, but some of them are shallow, weedy and unfrequented, requiring effort and perseverance on occasion. At the end of a day, as a result, you may feel a curious glow of achievement.

Though boat hiring, and pleasure boating generally, is rapidly increasing on canals, it is very much a post-war development and there are still very few pleasure boats per mile of waterway. You can often cruise all day and meet only one or two other craft, sometimes none at all. Thus, cruising on the canals is very different from Broads or Thames cruising. Whether you prefer it is largely a matter of temperament: the contrast is rather akin to that between a highly developed seaside resort with every holiday amenity and a small fishing village with none. It is a matter of taste.

These three—Broads, Thames and canals—provide the main market for holiday hire craft each year. There are, however, as mentioned earlier, various additional cruising grounds well worth consideration, and, indeed, the cruising addict will almost certainly go on from exploration of the popular waters to try these. The waterways of the Fens offer some lovely cruising, and several old-established (and some new) hire firms are based in these areas. The river Nene (Northampton, via Peterborough, to the Wash) is almost unknown to many, yet it is most attractive, and now has its own river-based hire fleet. To the west, the rivers Severn and (Warwickshire) Avon have their own character and charm, with hire fleets based on both. Holiday craft may also be hired on Windermere and elsewhere in the Lake District, offering the possibility of combining boating with walking in magnificent country. In addition, though beyond the scope of this book, mention should be made of the growth of pleasure cruising in Ireland, mainly on the Shannon, the Grand Canal and Lough Erne. Ireland is one of the last unspoiled countries in Europe (thanks to its climate), and offers wonderful boating to the enterprising skipper. Some previous experience is probably desirable, particularly on the Shannon, and indeed over 90 per cent of hirers of Irish holiday craft have had previous experience on the English waterways. Finally, there are the Continental waterways, and those of the United States and Canada.

Thus, the choice of cruising area is wide and the kind of cruising available differs considerably from area to area. How is the beginner to face the problems of deciding which area, which firm, which boat? The problem of which area is fairly simple. Enough has been said in earlier paragraphs to give a general outline of the difference between the various cruising grounds. The choice will be personal (or governed by factors such as distance from home) and, for the beginner making a first cruise, is not all that important. There will be other cruises in other years in other areas, and a first cruise is a magical experience in *any* area.

You have decided, then, to explore the waterways, either by hiring a boat (Chapter 6) or buying one (Chapter 7); you have studied the waterways map and read one or two books (Chapter 10), and now you are ready to plan your first cruise. Here are some points to consider:

1 Your cruising possibilities depend upon the width, length, draught and occasionally height of your proposed craft. If it is 6 ft 10 in beam or less, and 45 ft long or less, you can go almost anywhere that there is water to float you. If the beam is over 6 ft. 10 in you are limited to the Broads, rivers and broad canals marked as such on your map. With up to 10 ft 6 in beam, you can go anywhere on a broad waterway. Over that, you are excluded from the Great Ouse above Earith; over 12 ft 6 in from the Grand Union Canal main line above Braunston, and from the Old West River. Above 13 ft, from the Nene. Above 14 ft most of the canals are excluded, and you are left with the bigger rivers.

On the Fenland waterways, the ruling length is 45 ft; on some northern canals, 57 to 62 ft; if your draught is over 2 ft 6 in, and you intend to cruise on the canals, you had better make inquiries about your proposed route.

2 Don't plan to be madly energetic. The first rule of cruising is 'Take it gently.' There is no hurry. It is an Alice Through the Looking Glass world on the waterways, where the more you hurry, the less you achieve. It's the hardest lesson of all to learn. In practice, you will find that about 7 hours a day of actual cruising will be enough, after you've taken time for eating, pottering, chatting with lock-keepers and other boatmen, sitting in canal pubs, or exploring the neighbourhood. What distance you can cover in 7 hours depends upon several factors: the depth and state of the waterway, the number of locks, the traffic you meet, and your freedom from hold-up.

3 On still water, like a lake, your speed depends upon what your

3 (*Above*) Loaded narrow boats on the Grand Union at Braunston. In wide locks they travel abreast like this but must go separately through narrow ones; (*below*) British Waterways hire cruiser, a converted shortened narrow boat, emerges from a narrow lock on the Oxford.

4 (*Above*) The big leap: Jessop and Telford's breath-taking Pontcysyllte aqueduct carries the Llangollen Canal across the Dee valley. Note intrepid cruiser at left; (*below*) the little leap: cantilever bridge over the tail of a Staffs & Worcs Canal lock. Note gap for towrope to pass through, to save unhitching the horse.

engine will do, and on the depth of water. When you have brought your propeller down to about 18 in off the bottom you have reached your maximum practicable speed. To try to go faster only means waste of fuel, and possible damage from your screw hitting something. But on a canal, with limited width as well as depth, your speed depends upon the cross-sectional area (depth × width) of the canal in relation to that of your boat: depth for the reasons given above, cross-sectional area because the speed you can go forward depends upon how easily the water in front of you can get past your hull. The wider and deeper the canal in relation to the width and depth of your boat, the more easily it can do so. There is a speed limit of 4 mph on all British Waterways Board canals, but on some, like the Llangollen, you can only do about half that. Take 3 mph as a reasonable average on most canals.

On rivers, width is not often a worry, though some, like the Fenland's Wissey, are intriguingly narrow. Depth may also sometimes have to be watched. But you must add something for the speed of the current when running downstream, and subtract when coming up. If the river is in flood, you may find yourself moving very fast downstream, and making little headway up. Take 5 mph as a reasonable average; 6 mph is the normal limit on the Board's rivers; 5 mph on parts of the Broads.

4   Locks: Some people avoid locks when planning their cruises. This seems a pity. They are perfectly simple to work, give one some exercise, and are popular with the children.

On some of the big rivers and canals, you will find lock-keepers and probably mechanized locks. But on the smaller ones most used for pleasure cruising, you and your crew will work the locks—if there is a lock-keeper about, his job is only to see the job is done properly and water is not wasted.

Your speed through locks will depend on how many hands you have to help (for fast work you need one on the boat, two on the lock and, if there are a number of locks together, a fourth making the next lock ready), and on whether the lock is ready for you or not. Being ready means that the previous boat left it as you want to find it—empty if you are going up, full if you are going down. If you have to wait while you fill up or empty it before entering, you will take that much longer to pass it. It is quite possible to be through a lock in three minutes, but reckoning on some not being ready, having to wait for a boat to come out of others, and odd delays, assume ten minutes.

Four other factors could affect your timing: weed, rain, traffic and breakdown. In your planning allow half a day each week for the unexpected. As you get back nearer to base, so you can draw on your reserve time, on the argument that when you are nearly home you could complete the voyage by towing the boat from the bank if you had a last-minute breakdown.

Weed will not usually trouble you much on the more popular cruising canals. But if you explore those less used, especially late in the year, you may find weedy sections. Unless you have a weed-slipping propeller—and few craft have—you may find that you'll have to clear your propeller from time to time. With weed we can perhaps couple the odd thing that can get itself wrapped round the screw. Whether it does is mostly chance—though to coast through bridgeholes in neutral, so bringing the stern up, reduces the risk.

Rain no one can do anything about. Light rain hardly matters in cruising unless it goes on for too long, but heavy rain is different. Hence one must work out a schedule for one's cruise that allows something for delays due to the weather.

Traffic delays are not often serious. They occur mainly on canals, and because hirers all start and finish their hires on a Saturday. Therefore every Saturday afternoon boats set off from hirers' yards for a week's or a fortnight's cruising, and every Friday night they are returning to be near the yards for a run-in on Saturday morning. On some of the more popular canals, like the Llangollen, this leads to some delay at the entrance locks as boats all going the same way (and therefore needing the locks to be emptied again after each passage) all want to enter the canal on Saturday evening or Sunday morning. And again as they all want to leave. Such delays are not serious, however, except at bank holiday week-ends, but they should be remembered when working out a time-table. Having taken all these into consideration, and remembered to allow for the unexpected, you will probably conclude that about sixteen miles and ten locks is a reasonable day's run on a narrow canal, reckoning 3 mph and 10 minutes for each lock: that is, 7 hours of cruising, to which we can add 1 hour for unexpected delays, making 8 hours in all. On broad canals and small rivers, you can raise the speed to 4 mph and the lock times to $12\frac{1}{2}$ minutes, on the bigger rivers to 5 mph and 15 minutes per lock. Reckon 5 mph for the Broads.

If you are hiring by the week, you have six full days, plus a little cruising on the first Saturday afternoon and evening to get away from the others, and a short run-in the following Saturday morning. Say about 90 miles and 60 locks. If your route includes river stretches, or some of the bigger canals, then up to 125 miles. Now you can work out a possible route. If it contains more locks than 60, deduct a mile for every two locks; if less, add a mile for every two locks. Such an arithmetical result is not a rule, but a guide—if you decide to attempt more, then you will know what to plan for; if less, you will know you will have more time for exploring and lazing.

The map will give you the position and number of locks, and you can judge waterway lengths from the scale; the suggestions that follow later in this chapter give most of the lengths; *The Canals Book* has much of the detail. Having worked out some provisional ideas, get the BWB Inland Cruising Booklets or similar publications for your chosen area, anything your boatyard provides for you, and also the 1-in Ordnance maps, and then do the rest of your planning.

Here are some things to decide upon:

(a) Do you want a circular cruise, or are you quite happy to go there and back? The one gives you the maximum of new scenes, the other the pleasure of revisiting those that pleased you on the way up. If you have bought a boat, there is also the possibility of cruising in instalments; boating for a week-end, leaving the craft under someone's eye, going home by car or rail, and returning next week-end to do another lap.

If you are making a circular cruise, try if possible to do the hardest part of the route first, giving you the easiest part for the return journey. This enables you much more easily to make up lost time if necessary. If your route is an out-and-back cruise along the same waterway, try to plan your meal and night stops at different places on the out and return journeys. The waterway seems quite different when seen in reverse on the return journey so that out-and-back trips are just as interesting as circular routes. And they do offer the added advantage that you can, if you specially want to, pay a return visit to a particularly attractive mooring.

(b) *Seasons*

The popular months for cruising are from mid-June to mid-September. But if you are hiring, craft are of course then more expensive. We ourselves like April or May cruising. These months are usually dry; there is a freshness about the country that compensates for the lack of leaves on the trees; hiring is cheap; boats and engines have had a winter overhaul and are newly out of the yards; and the less-used waterways are free of weed. There is much to be said, on the other hand, for late September or October. The mist of early morning, autumn colour of the trees and brown leaves floating on the water, reeds turning to gold, the smell of wood-smoke.

(c) *Fuel*

Most hire craft carry enough fuel for a week, so you have not got to worry. But there are canals, like the Leicester line between Norton junction and Foxton, with few fuelling points, so plan not to run low.

(d) *Shopping and Mail*

If you are hiring, you will start with a full load of groceries that will carry you over Sunday. But after that, plan where you are going to shop, and do not forget early closing days. You can also work out *poste restante* addresses for mail, but allow for the possibility that you may run early on your schedule.

(e) *Moorings for the Night*

You will probably want to be near a road, for shopping and in case friends want to find you, and a pub after all the work you will have done. From the Cruising Booklets and the Ordnance map you can make provisional choices; if you do not reach them, no great harm is done. Remember that if you are hiring, your first night will probably have to be spent within about six miles of the base, and your last within two or three.

(f) Most lock flights and tunnels are open from 8 am to 7 pm seven days a week; there are a few exceptions: ask your hirer or club.

(g) *Stoppages*

From time to time the navigation authority has to close a lock for two or three days to put in new gates or repair the chamber. On the main cruising canals these are as far as possible scheduled for the winter, but some stoppages have to be made. Your hiring firm, boat club or canal society will have a list of places and dates, or you can write to British Waterways for copies of the annual Stoppage Programme, issued in two sections, for the northern and southern regions.

(h) If you are hiring, check with your hiring firm about three weeks ahead of your cruise that the tour you have chosen is practicable for the boat you are having (width for narrow canals, height for a few low bridges or tunnels), and that there are no stoppages on your route. This gives you time to replan. If you intend to touch tidal waters at any point, check that the hiring firm agrees that you may— insurance policies often prohibit it.

(i) *Waterway Charges*

If you are hiring a craft, licence fees payable to the local waterway authority will be included in the hire charge. If you move on to the waters of a different authority, for instance, from British Waterways Board water to those of others you may be covered by reciprocal arrangements, or you may have to pay a charge. Ask your hirer.

If you are buying a boat, find out licence and toll charges from the authority on whose waters you will be cruising. Names and addresses are given in the *Canal Enthusiasts' Handbook*.

With your voyage planned in advance, you should always know what lies ahead each day when you cast off. If you are in doubt about anything never hesitate to ask local help. Lock-keepers and other boatmen will always give you information and advice and nobody ever thinks the worse of you for asking for advice if you know there's a tricky bit of navigation ahead or are not sure, for example, exactly where the next lock cut turns out of the main stream of the river.

One last point: If your cruise is a family affair, remember that steering the boat may be a wonderful change from working in the office or factory for you, but cooking and washing up on a boat isn't all that much of a change for your wife. So try to organize it so that everyone takes a hand at all the chores—the skipper included. And don't assume that because your wife can't drive the family car she necessarily can't handle the boat either. Boatyards who are used to novice hirers know very well that very often the non-driver makes the better helmsman and the wives, more ready to listen to professional advice, often make better helmsmen than their husbands. Truth to tell, the husbands often secretly think that there's really nothing to handling a boat and that all men can do it well instinctively. If you share the jobs, everyone gets a change and everyone gets a holiday.

And so—where to go? The possibilities are endless. Here are some suggestions, which you can follow on the map in this book:

CIRCULAR CRUISES

These can of course be started anywhere on the circle.
1 Stourport down the Severn to Worcester; Worcester & Birmingham Canal to Worcester Bar, Birmingham; Birmingham Canal main line to Dudley Port; thence by Netherton tunnel

branch and old Dudley Canal to Stourbridge Canal to Stourton; then Staffs & Worcs Canal to Stourport.
79 miles, 4 Severn locks, 2 broad locks, 101 narrow locks. All British Waterways Board.

2 Stourport down the Severn to Worcester; Worcester & Birmingham Canal to Worcester Bar, Birmingham; Birmingham Canal main line to Aldersley, then Staffs & Worcs Canal back to Stourport.
84½ miles, 4 Severn locks, 2 broad locks, 111 narrow locks. All BWB.

3 Braunston via Grand Union to Birmingham, Bordesley Junc; to Salford Bridge; then by Birmingham & Fazeley Canal to Fazeley; Coventry Canal to Hawkesbury; Oxford Canal to Braunston.
100 miles, 51 broad locks, 40 narrow locks. BWB.

4 Middlewich to Barbridge Junction; Shropshire Union main line to Autherley; Staffs & Worcs to Great Haywood; Trent & Mersey Canal to Middlewich.
108½ miles, 89 narrow locks. All BWB.

5 Braunston to Norton Junction; Leicester line via Leicester to Trent Junction; River Trent and Trent & Mersey Canal to Fradley; Coventry Canal to Hawkesbury; Oxford Canal to Braunston.
129½ miles, 55 broad locks, 45 narrow locks. All BWB.

6 Middlewich to Barbridge Junction; Shropshire Union main line to Autherley; via Birmingham Canal main line to Farmer's Bridge; Birmingham & Fazeley Canal and Coventry Canal to Fradley; Trent & Mersey Canal to Middlewich.
143 miles, 120 narrow locks. All BWB.

7 Oxford by River Thames to Brentford; Grand Union Canal to Braunston; Oxford Canal to Oxford.
249 miles, 33 Thames locks, 101 broad locks, 39 narrow locks. Thames Conservancy, Oxford–Teddington. No toll, Teddington–Brentford. Thence BWB.

8 *The Little Circle.* Middlewich by Trent & Mersey Canal to Derwent Mouth; River Trent via Gainsborough to Keadby; Stainforth & Keadby Canal to Bramwith; New Junction Canal; Aire & Calder to Leeds; Leeds & Liverpool Canal via Wigan to Leigh; Bridgewater Canal via Stretford Junction to Preston Brook; Trent & Mersey to Middlewich.

354½ miles, 121 broad locks, 68 narrow locks. All BWB except Gainsborough–Keadby (toll-free), and Leigh–Preston Brook (Bridgewater Dept, Manchester Ship Canal Co). Tidal, Cromwell lock to Keadby.

9 *The Great Circle.* Braunston by Grand Union to Norton Junction, thence by Leicester line to Trent Junction; River Trent via Beeston Cut to Nottingham, and on via Gainsborough to Keadby; Stainforth & Keadby Canal to Bramwith; New Junction Canal; Aire & Calder to Leeds; Leeds & Liverpool Canal via Wigan to Leigh; Bridgewater Canal via Stretford Junction to Preston Brook; Trent & Mersey Canal to Middlewich; thence to Barbridge Junction; Shropshire Union main line to Autherley; Birmingham Canal main line to Farmer's Bridge; thence via Ashted locks to the Grand Union at Bordesley; Grand Union to Braunston. Tidal, Cromwell lock to Keadby.
458 miles, 219 broad locks, 96 narrow locks.
Alternative from Middlewich, continue up Trent & Mersey to Fradley; Coventry Canal to Hawkesbury; Oxford Canal to Braunston.
453 miles, 168 broad locks, 85 narrow locks. All BWB except Gainsborough–Keadby, toll-free, and Leigh–Preston Brook, Bridgewater Dept, Manchester Ship Canal Co.

THERE AND BACK

The following suggested trips can, of course, be shortened (in some cases lengthened), reversed, or combined, as desired. Distances and numbers of locks are for a *return* journey.

1 Braunston via the Oxford Canal to Oxford.
110 miles, 76 narrow locks. All BWB.
2 Braunston to Lechlade via the Oxford Canal and River Thames.
137 miles, 18 Thames locks, 76 narrow locks. BWB to Oxford, thence Thames Conservancy.
3 Braunston to Stratford-upon-Avon, via the Grand Union and Stratford Canals.
79 miles, 92 broad, 58 narrow locks. BWB to Kingswood Junction, then National Trust.

4 Braunston to Ashby Canal head, via the Oxford, Coventry and Ashby Canals.
92 miles, 6 narrow locks. All BWB.

5 Braunston to Market Harborough, via the Grand Union and the Leicester line.
66 miles, 12 broad, 34 narrow locks. All BWB.

6 Braunston to Welford Lock, via the Grand Union and the Leicester line.
42 miles, 12 broad, 14 narrow locks. All BWB.

7 Braunston to Fenny Stratford (Bletchley), via the Grand Union.
77 miles, 44 broad locks. All BWB.

8 Braunston to Fotheringhay, via the Grand Union, the Northampton branch and the River Nene.
129 miles, 86 broad, 34 narrow locks. BWB to Northampton, thence Welland & Nene River Authority.
(For the connexion via the Middle Level to the Fenland waterways see p 48.)

9 Stourport to Sharpness, via River Severn and Gloucester & Berkeley (Sharpness) Canal.
118 miles, 12 Severn locks. All BWB.

10 Stourport to Evesham, via River Severn and Lower Avon.
116 miles, 8 Severn locks, 18 broad locks. BWB to Tewkesbury, then Lower Avon Navigation Trust.

11 Stourport to Stoke Wharf, via River Severn and Worcester & Birmingham Canal.
54 miles, 6 Severn, 8 broad, 40 narrow locks. All BWB.

12 Stourport to Gailey, via the Staffs & Worcs Canal.
64 miles, 58 narrow locks. All BWB.

13 Stourport to Market Drayton, via the Staffs & Worcs and Shropshire Union Canals.
103 miles, 72 narrow locks. All BWB.

14 Stourport to Blowers Green (to see Dudley tunnel), via the Staffs & Worcs, Stourbridge and Dudley canals.
40 miles, 80 narrow locks. All BWB.

15 Middlewich to Llangollen, via the Middlewich branch, Shropshire Union main line, and Llangollen Canal.
112 miles, 50 narrow locks. All BWB.

16 Middlewich to Chester, via the Middlewich branch and Shropshire Union.
52 miles, 28 broad, 8 narrow locks. All BWB.

17 Middlewich–Stone, via the Trent & Mersey Canal.
54 miles, 90 narrow locks. All BWB.

18 Middlewich–Hazelhurst, via Trent & Mersey and Caldon branch.
55 miles, 80 narrow locks. (Inquire from BWB state of Caldon branch first.) All BWB.

19 Middlewich–Whaley Bridge, via Trent & Mersey, Macclesfield and Upper Peak Forest Canals.
90 miles, 86 narrow locks. All BWB.

20 Middlewich–Weston Marsh via Trent & Mersey, Anderton lift, and River Weaver.
44 miles, 2 lift, 8 broad, 6 narrow locks. All BWB. (Special return charge for lift.)

21 Middlewich–Runcorn via Trent & Mersey and Bridgewater Canal.
45 miles, 4 broad, 6 narrow locks. BWB to Preston Brook, thence Bridgewater Dept, Manchester Ship Canal Co.

22 Middlewich–Johnson's Hillock, via the Trent & Mersey, Bridgewater, and Leeds & Liverpool Canals.
136½ miles, 50 broad, 6 narrow locks. All BWB except Preston Brook–Leigh, Bridgewater Dept, Manchester Ship Canal.

23 Middlewich to Scarisbrick, via the Trent & Mersey, Bridgewater and Leeds & Liverpool Canals.
142 miles, 16 broad, 6 narrow locks. All BWB except Preston Brook–Leigh, Bridgewater Dept, Manchester Ship Canal Co.

24 Nottingham to Market Harborough, via the River Trent and the Leicester line.
116 miles, 94 broad locks. All BWB.

25 Nottingham to Lincoln, via the River Trent and the Fossdyke. Part tidal.
109 miles, 14 Trent locks, 2 broad locks. All BWB.

26 Nottingham to Boston, via the River Trent, the Fossdyke and the River Witham. Part tidal.
154 miles, 14 Trent locks, 6 broad locks. All BWB.
(There is an alternative route to Boston via Guthram Gowt Lock on the Witham.*)

27 Nottingham to Retford, via the River Trent and the Chesterfield Canal. Part tidal.

* By taking a pilot at Boston, it is possible to enter the Welland which is navigable to Crowland.

150 miles, 14 Trent locks, 14 broad locks. All BWB except Gainsborough–West Stockwith, toll-free under 5 tons.

28 Nottingham to Bramwith, via the River Trent and the Stainforth and Keadby Canal. Part tidal.
230 miles, 14 Trent locks, 4 broad locks. All BWB except Gainsborough–Keadby, toll-free under 5 tons

29 Kingston Bridge to Lechlade. River Thames.
242 miles, 86 Thames locks. All Thames Conservancy.

30 Kingston Bridge to Oxford, River Thames.
183 miles, 62 Thames locks. All Thames Conservancy.

31 Kingston Bridge to Wallingford, River Thames.
140½ miles, 48 Thames locks. All Thames Conservancy.

32 Kingston Bridge to Newbury, via River Thames and Kennet & Avon Canal (not at present fully navigable).
143 miles, 38 Thames locks, 42 broad locks. (Inquire from BWB state of Kennet & Avon first.) Thames Conservancy to Reading, then BWB.

33 Kingston Bridge to Sonning, River Thames.
101½ miles, 36 Thames locks. All Thames Conservancy.

34 Kingston Bridge to Maidenhead, River Thames.
58½ miles, 20 Thames locks. All Thames Conservancy.

35 Kingston Bridge to Guildford, via River Thames and River Wey.
49½ miles, 6 Thames locks, 24 broad locks. Inquire about bridge clearance. Thames Conservancy to Weybridge, then National Trust.

36 Kingston Bridge to Godalming, via River Thames and River Wey.
58 miles, 6 Thames locks, 32 broad locks. Inquire about bridge clearance. Thames Conservancy to Weybridge, then National Trust.

37 Waltham Town Lock to Hertford, River Lee.
26½ miles, 20 broad locks. All BWB.

38 Waltham Town Lock to Bishop's Stortford, via River Lee and River Stort.
39 miles, 42 broad locks. Bridge clearance 6 ft 3 in. All BWB.

39 Maidstone to Tonbridge, River Medway.
32 miles, 18 locks. Kent River Authority.

40 Brecon Canal. Open Pontypool to Brecon, 64 miles return.
10 narrow locks. All BWB.

41 Lancaster Canal, main line return.
84 miles, no locks; branch to Glasson dock, 5 miles return, 12 broad locks. All BWB.

42 York–Boroughbridge, via River Ouse.
42 miles, 4 broad locks. York to Widdington Ings, Ouse Navigation Trustees; Widdington Ings to Swale Nab, Linton Lock Commissioners; Swale Nab upwards, BWB.

43 York to Sowerby Bridge, via the River Ouse, Selby Canal, Aire & Calder and Calder & Hebble Navigations. Part tidal.
135 miles, 100 broad locks. Yorks Ouse Nav Trustees to Selby, thence BWB.

44 York to Skipton, via the River Ouse, Selby Canal, Aire & Calder and Leeds & Liverpool Canal. Part tidal.
154 miles, 86 broad locks. Yorks Ouse Nav Trustees to Selby, thence BWB.

45 York to Barrowford, via the River Ouse, Selby Canal, Aire & Calder and Leeds & Liverpool Canal. Part tidal.
189 miles, 116 broad locks. Yorks Ouse Nav Trustees to Selby, thence BWB.

46 *The Broads.* The northern part of this cruising area consists of the rivers Bure, Ant and Thurne with their accompanying broads (lakes), the southern of the rivers Yare and Waveney, the two parts coming together at Yarmouth. They represent about 200 miles of cruising, and can all be explored in a week if you feel that energetic. The area is, of course, self-contained unless you enter it from the sea. The main centres are Wroxham and Horning on the Bure, Potter Heigham on the Thurne, Yarmouth, Oulton Broad near Lowestoft, and Beccles on the Waveney, but craft can be hired at many others (see *The Broads Book*). Much of the area is tidal, and money can be saved if a cruise is planned to take advantage of the tide. Distances are: Coltishall, the upper navigable limit of the Bure, to Beccles, on the Waveney, 52 miles; Norwich to Yarmouth 27½ miles.

47 About 150 miles of Fenland waterways, with very few locks, are available to cruisers. The upper limit of navigation on the Great Ouse is at Tempsford Bridge on the Great North Road. Downwards from here you cruise through pretty rural scenery past St Neots, Godmanchester, Huntingdon and St Ives to Earith. Then to your left is the uninteresting 21 dead-straight

miles of the tidal New Bedford River leading to the Ouse just below Denver Sluice; it is not recommended. To your right, through Hermitage Lock, is the pretty Old West River to Pope's Corner, whence the Cam River comes in on your right. (The section between Brownshill Lock, just above Earith, and Hermitage Lock, just below it, is tidal.) You can cruise up the Cam to Cambridge, exploring Burwell and Reach Lodes on the way. Continuing down the Ouse past Ely, you can turn up the Lark to Judes Ferry, the Little Ouse to near Brandon, or the delightful Wissey to Stoke Ferry. Beyond the junction with the Wissey is the end of the cruising area at Denver Sluice. You can pass the lock into the tidal river if you wish to turn left into the New Bedford River back to Earith, but the lower Great Ouse is not open to hire craft. The main cruising bases for the Fenland waterways are Cambridge, Ely, St Ives, Huntingdon and Earith: for the Nene at Oundle.

It is possible, but not easy, to get from the Nene, and so from the canal system, into the Fenland waterways, by several different routes through the Middle Level, especially in April to June, before weed growth gets bad. Those who want to try should seek the advice of the East Anglian Waterways Association (see also the article on the Middle Level in *The Fens Book*).

GOING OVERSEAS

After you have done a few cruises in Britain, you may like to look abroad.

There is Ireland. Three suggestions are:

(a) Upper and Lower Lough Erne, mainly in Northern Ireland; 52 miles long, with 365 islands. Hire cruiser bases, Enniskillen (NI), Belturbet (Eire).

(b) The Shannon, Eire, 128 miles of river and lake from Limerick to Battlebridge; 6 locks. Hire cruiser bases at Killaloe, Athlone, Roosky, Carrick-on-Shannon, Coothall, etc.

(c) Grand Canal and Barrow Navigation, Eire. Grand Canal, Dublin to the Shannon 34 miles upstream from Limerick; 82 miles long, 36 locks. The Barrow line leaves the canal 30 miles from Dublin and stretches for 70 miles through 23 locks to the sea-lock at St Mullins. Hire cruiser bases at Shannon Harbour on the Grand Canal, Carlow on the Barrow.

Then there is Europe. For background, read Roger Pilkington's books (see p 146). *Small Boat Through Belgium* contains his account of how he took his cruiser across the Channel. This is one way of doing it—another is to hire abroad.

Motor-boating on inland waterways, and especially on canals, rather than on the sea, is little developed on the Continent, but you can hire craft in the Netherlands and also in France, where the boom is just beginning, one firm there being British. It is very different in the United States and Canada: there is ample scope for motor-boating on rivers and canals in both countries.

CHAPTER FOUR

Under Way

Handling a boat isn't really very much like driving a car, and even the controls are different. The biggest difference, however, is not in the controls but in the fact that a car will keep still if you stop it, whereas a boat won't, and a car will normally only move forward or backwards in the direction in which it is steered, whereas a boat will move sideways as well.

STEERING

Let's look at the controls first. A boat is steered either by a wheel or by a tiller, connected to a rudder. When you turn the wheel or move the tiller you move the rudder to one side or the other. The rudder is placed immediately behind the propeller so that the 'slipstream' of water from the propeller plays on to it. When you turn the rudder, the slipstream is deflected to one side or the other and this tends to cause the rear of the boat to move to one side or the other. Even if the propeller is not turning, the boat will still answer to the rudder if it is moving in relation to the water, but not otherwise. In other words, you will not steer if you are drifting at the same speed as moving water, no matter how fast you may be passing the bank. You must have steerage way relative to the water for the rudder to work.

If your power unit is an outboard motor the steering effect is achieved not by deflecting the propeller stream by a rudder, but by swivelling the whole outboard unit and thereby altering the direction of the thrust. Some outboard motors have rudder units attached as well, but these are only to give steering when moving at very low speeds.

You will notice from this that whereas turning the steering-wheel of a car causes the front wheels to turn, so that the front of the car changes direction with the rest of the car following, turning the rudder of a boat causes the back—the stern—to move to one side or the other. In fact, when you alter course in a boat, the stern moves one way and the bow moves the other, the pivot point being somewhere amidships. This is one of the most important things to remember. If you park your car close to a kerb you can drive away quite easily by simply turning the steering-wheel. The front wheels immediately pull away from the kerb and the rest of the car will follow. But if your boat is close to a wall you cannot simply turn the wheel and steer away because the stern will try to move *into* the wall before the bow can swing away. You must either push the bow out and steer away in a straight line or push the whole boat out to give the stern room to swing in as the bow swings away.

Most people find difficulty in steering a straight course to begin with, and oversteer wildly so that the boat swings alarmingly from side to side. This is caused by over-correcting errors and can be cured quite simply. *Never* watch the bow of the boat directly, any more than you would watch the bonnet of a car on the open road. Stare ahead at the distant scenery, keeping the wheel or tiller quite still. When the boat begins to swing off course you will see the bow begin to move to one side or the other out of the corner of your eye. When this begins, move the wheel or tiller gently against the swing, and as soon as you see that the swing is stopping *keep the wheel still*. If you have over-corrected, the boat will begin gently to swing the other way. Again, make a gentle correction and as soon as you see that this is having an effect, hold the wheel still. Within a moment, the swinging will have stopped and you should then be able to control the boat with only

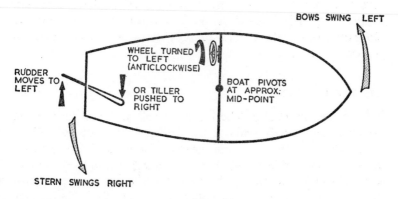

FIG 1   How a boat steers

51

the smallest movement of wheel or tiller. Remember to stare ahead and watch the boat only out of the corner of your eye as the bow swings across the distant view, and remember to use minimum wheel movements and to hold still until the swing is corrected.

Two other points in connexion with steering are that a boat won't keep still when it's stopped and that it will have a tendency to drift sideways. It won't keep still because of current in the water or wind or both, so you will generally need to keep a little way on to give control. Generally, it is best to avoid having to try to keep stationary. If you are coming up to a lock that isn't ready or a swing bridge that isn't open, slow down and keep creeping along under control instead of batting up at full bore and then having to try to hold the boat in one place for any length of time. It can be done, of course, but it takes practice and you are wisest to avoid it where possible. Sideways drift is not normally a problem with an inboard boat with a keel and rudder, but it can make handling a shallow draught outboard cruiser tricky. The deeper the boat in the water, the more 'grip' it has and therefore the less tendency to slide sideways. Allowing for lateral drift is something which comes with experience.

Steering in reverse often needs a moment's thought, to decide which way to put the wheel or tiller. Work it out on the basis that the rudder itself must point in the direction you wish to go. But it is often quite difficult, and some boats will hardly steer at all when going backwards. If you find that yours does not respond to the wheel when in reverse, the only thing you can do is to go into forward gear occasionally to straighten up and get the stern pointing in the right direction. There is no short cut here, and only practice will make perfect. Outboard boats, of course, steer as well backwards as forwards, since the pivoting of the motor simply pulls the whole boat in the required direction.

THE ENGINE CONTROLS

So much for steering. The other controls are two: the throttle, nearly always a small hand-operated lever, and the gear lever. There is no clutch control on a marine gearbox. Sometimes these two controls are combined in a single lever, which is very simple. All you do then is push the lever in the direction in which you wish to travel—forwards or backwards. The initial movement of the single lever selects the gear, and the rest of the travel opens the throttle. If there

5 (*Above*) Locks are the usual way of taking a canal uphill: here's another—the Anderton lift near Northwich. Two enormous tanks rise and fall 50 ft between the river Weaver and the Trent & Mersey Canal; (*below*) If canals couldn't go over hills they went through them. The southern entrance to Harecastle tunnel on the Trent & Mersey. The squared opening is for doors to close the tunnel for forced ventilation; the curved gauge indicates maximum headroom at midpoint where the tunnel has subsided.

6 (*Above*) Locks are usually encountered one at a time. Here at Bingley on the Leeds & Liverpool Canal five come together in an unusual 'staircase'; (*below*) most locks have traditional wooden gates at each end. On the river Nene in Northamptonshire these vertical steel guillotines take the place of the lower gates.

are two levers, all you do is to shove the gear lever forward or astern and work the separate throttle to give the required speed. The only rule is that you should slow down to idling speed before moving the lever.

What about brakes? Of course there aren't any on a boat. So how do you stop? Normally, you know well in advance where you want to stop, and you slow down in good time, come into neutral (ie out of gear) and allow the diminishing momentum of the boat to carry you to where you want to stop. If you 'undershoot' and don't quite get there you give 'a little touch ahead' to give you a bit more way forward. If you overshoot, and arrive too fast, or if you have to stop in a panic, you simply go into reverse, gently or hard according to the circumstances, until all forward motion ceases, and then into neutral again before the boat starts gathering way astern. Apart from emergencies, however, it is a sign of sloppy boating to have to go hard astern to stop your boat. With a little practice you should be able to judge it so that the merest touch of astern is all that is needed to bring you to rest.

A FEW TECHNICAL TERMS

So much for the controls. A few technical terms may be useful: bow or bows—the front of the boat. Forward—towards the bows. Aft—towards the back, or stern. Amidships—in the middle of the boat. Transom—the square stern end of the boat. Bilges—inside the bottom of the boat under the floorboards. Rubbing strakes—protective strips along the sides to save the hull from chafing on locksides, etc. Cleats—T-shaped deck fittings for attaching mooring lines. Fairleads—guides through which mooring lines are passed to keep them from chafing the edge of the decks. Port—left-hand side (red light); starboard—right-hand side (green light). (Easy mnemonic: the ship LEFT the PORT—PORT wine is RED). On most British Waterways Board canals, you must show a white light forward, usually a headlight, if you move at night; on some bigger waterways, as on the Broads and the Thames, you must show proper navigation lights after dark.

STARTING OFF

And now, with the theory safely out of the way, let's get started on

D 55

a typical day's cruise and take the problems as they present themselves. First of all, and this really is first of all, get the children into buoyancy jackets. The chances are that they won't be the ones to fall in—children are much more sure-footed than their parents—but mother's shout of 'be careful' can sometimes catch a child off balance and cause it to miss its footing. Most hire firms offer buoyancy jackets for children on free loan. Make sure you get them. If it is your own boat, fit each child with his own buoyancy jacket and *insist* that it is worn from first thing in the morning until last thing at night. If any of the adults in your crew are non-swimmers, put them in jackets as well as a counsel of perfection: failing this, make sure you have a lifebuoy handy at all times to throw to anyone who falls in. On canals the risk of an adult drowning is very slight indeed, as very few strokes are needed to reach shallow water. It is different on rivers and Broads and there's nothing 'chicken' about wearing a buoyancy jacket—it's a sensible routine precaution on a par with the motor cyclist's crash helmet or the airman's parachute. By the same token, particularly if it's your own boat and you are going to spend a good deal of time afloat, invest a little time in studying life-saving procedures and methods of resuscitation. Many a life has been lost unnecessarily for the lack of someone on the scene with the knowledge to do the right thing *quickly*. Your local Ambulance Brigade will tell you where you can obtain instruction, and if a few evenings of study one day enable you to save a life you will count the time well spent.

ROUTINE MAINTENANCE

With your crew safely buoyant and as the time for casting off and starting the day's cruise approaches, carry out your routine daily maintenance. Check your fuel tank and fill this from your spare cans. Refill these as soon as possible. (No smoking and cooking stove off during refuelling.) Check your water tanks. Have a good look at your engine to make sure that everything appears in order, with nothing working loose. Dip the oil levels in the sump and gearbox and top up as necessary. Carry out any required lubrication: usually a turn on the water-pump greaser and on the greaser on the stern gland—where the propeller shaft passes out through the bottom of the boat. Check the bilges for water and pump out if necessary. If there seems to be excessive bilge water, find out why. While you have the floorboards up or the engine case open, start the engine and let it run in neutral while you have a look all round it. Any sign of water leaking from cooling pipes? Any sign of oil leaking anywhere? Anything rattling or vibrating that needs to be tightened up? Have a look over the stern or side and check that the cooling water is coming through properly. If everything seems in order, put down the floorboards, close the engine case, and you're ready to cast off. This sort of check takes only a few minutes each day and by giving you an early warning of anything going wrong amply repays you for the time it takes.

Running the engine for a few moments before you cast off your ropes gives it a chance to warm up so that when you do engage forward gear it is unlikely to stall. There's nothing sillier than that, particularly on a flowing river, where you drift helplessly away pushing at the starter button and cursing and providing free entertainment for the locals.

With your engine ticking over, make sure that everything (and everyone) is on board. If you have a raised canopy and are cruising on waters with low bridges, take this down and stow it properly. Stow away all loose gear that may have been placed on cabin tops or decks while you were moored. Make sure your boathook is handy. If you were moored to your own mooring pegs or rond anchors, haul these up, clean the mud off them and stow them aboard. Mooring ropes should be coiled neatly and put where they cannot fall overboard and get wound round your propeller. Coil ropes clockwise, starting near the fixed end and leaving the loose end to rotate as you coil them up. If you coil anti-clockwise you are working against the 'lay' of the strands of the rope, and it won't coil sweetly. If you coil from the loose end it can't rotate and will simply snarl up on you. *Always* have your ropes properly coiled and ready for instant use when you are cruising—you may need them in an emergency when there's no time to start untangling a mess.

CASTING OFF

In still waters, you can untie either end first, and simply push off from the bank into deeper water before engaging gear and moving off. In rivers with any appreciable current, you should untie the stern end (assuming you have moored correctly, bows upstream) first, and then untie the bow and push off when you are ready to go.

Unless you are certain that the water is deep right into your mooring, always push the stern out and reverse away from the bank into deep water before starting forward. This saves your propeller from the risk of fouling submerged stones.

It is important to realise that inland waterways are often quite shallow at the edges. There is a navigable channel which usually runs up the centre on straight lengths and swings towards the outside of bends. This is true of rivers and most canals, although some busy commercial waterways have both banks piled for protection and are deep dredged for their full width.

THE ENGINE INSTRUMENTS

When you are under way safely, have a look at your instruments. Usually these will consist of a minimum of oil pressure gauge, thermometer and ammeter. Oil pressure should stay steady: a sudden drop indicates trouble and you should stop engine and find out what has gone wrong. Temperature should also stay fairly steady, though it may hunt up and down a little as the thermostat opens and closes on the engine. Here a sudden rise is the danger signal. Again, stop and find out why. The most likely cause of overheating is weed sucked into the inlet strainer and blocking it. The ammeter shows that the engine is recharging your batteries. It will probably show quite a substantial rate of charge first of all, but this will gradually fall away as the batteries 'fill up' and the automatic control reduces the charge to save them from damage caused by over-charging.

USE YOUR EARS

Apart from a visual check on your instruments from time to time, use your ears to detect any sudden change in engine note or sudden vibration. On most inboard engines the cooling water is discharged through the exhaust pipe, cooling the pipe and helping to silence the engine. If the cooling flow stops through weed blockage or other cause, the engine note will change immediately, from a happy gurgling to a harsher note. If the engine noise changes, find out why. It could be a warning of trouble on the way. Similarly with vibration, suddenly apparent: this is a warning of something wrong—most commonly weed or rope or sacking caught up in the prop and thrashing round with it. (We'll deal with this problem a little later.) Finally, use your nose. If you don't see the temperature gauge swing to H and beyond and don't hear the exhaust note alter you'll still smell an overheating engine very quickly. Don't ignore sudden wafts of burning rubber or overheated metal—it may just be the lunch going wrong or it may be a danger signal. Find out. The good boatman (like the good driver or pilot) has his three senses constantly tuned to detect any *change* without consciously thinking about it.

KEEPING A LOOK-OUT

When you are cruising along, keep a good look-out generally. Keep your eyes on your own crew, particularly on children and unless there's someone else on deck to watch them never let them get out of your sight behind you on deck. By all means let them sit on the foredeck where you can see them but never down aft. If they fall off the bow you will see them fall: if they fall off astern it could be half an hour before you even missed them. Keep a look-out not only for other craft approaching but also for faster craft coming up from behind, and watch the water ahead for obstructions, driftwood and swimmers.

SPEED

Make sure that you do not exceed the permitted speed for the area. Waterway authorities rightly clamp down hard on craft which ignore such restrictions and ignorance of the law is no defence. If in doubt ask someone or go slowly. In any case, you should never proceed along a narrow waterway at such a speed as to drag a breaking wave along the bank behind you. This not only damages the banks, but also wastes your petrol, and you should throttle down until your wash is no more than a gentle undulation. If you are causing a breaking wave on one bank but not on the other, then you are not in the centre of the channel. Move away from the side where the wave is breaking until it stops.

Other circumstances in which you should slow down and avoid making more than an absolute minimum of wash are when meeting or overtaking small craft—rowing boats, canoes and the like—and when passing dredgers and bank maintenance craft at work. Finally, you should always slow down before passing craft moored alongside. There is good reason for this as you will find out for yourself if some lout charges past your own boat without slowing down when you are moored up in a peaceful spot. His wash will rock you violently and cause you to surge backwards and forwards. Externally this can damage your boat by causing it to bash into the bank or by thumping it on the bottom between waves if the mooring is shallow. It can snatch and break fender lanyards and mooring ropes, or drag mooring stakes out of the ground. Inside, china and pans can slide off shelves, tables and cooker—and if there happens to be a kettle or pan boiling and a small child passing at the same moment it can cause a serious accident. Thoughtlessness in passing moored craft causes more bad feeling than anything else and is quite unforgivable. Finally, watch out for anglers peacefully fishing from the towpath. Try to disturb them as little as possible. Keep to the far bank to avoid their tackle (which is often expensive), and slow down so that your wash is not offensive.

MEETING AND PASSING

It is worth noting that if you happen to meet loaded barges or narrow boats in a bend the normal rule of passing—keep right—may not be the wisest course. If it is a left-hand bend for you, keeping to the right would put you outside the oncoming heavy craft, between them and the bank they are hugging. Since your pleasure craft will almost certainly draw less water than they require, the barge skipper will probably wave to you to keep to your left and pass him on the inside, leaving the deeper water for him. If this happens, alter course immediately and obviously, even making a clear hand signal to indicate that you have understood. Do not make the mistake of going too far towards the inside of the bend in these circumstances or, again, you may run aground. Keep as close to him as is safe and sensible.

Normally, of course, the rule for passing is Keep Right and this should always be followed except in special circumstances. Do not make the mistake, when meeting another boat, of going so far to the right that you get into shallow water near the bank. Each approaching skipper needs merely to alter course a little to allow for the two craft to pass with several feet between. On canals you will need to pass much closer to oncoming craft than on wider, deeper rivers and Broads.

On waterways with heavy commercial traffic, approaching working craft may indicate their intended course by sound signals from their hooter. One toot means 'I am altering course to starboard' (I am keeping right); two toots means keeping left; three means 'My engines are going astern', four 'I am about to turn round'—if followed after a pause by one toot, then to starboard (right); if by two toots, to port (left). If you are meeting a boat and expecting him to keep right and he suddenly gives two toots and swings to his left (perhaps he is going in to a wharf) you should reply with a similar signal and clearly be seen to alter course accordingly.

Do not be alarmed by all this, however. Ninety-nine times out of every hundred the normal rule applies and two craft simply pass each other with as little fuss as two cars passing on a road.

OVERTAKING

In overtaking, the rule is the same—you keep right as a general rule. However, it is worth remembering that the overtaken boat is not under any obligation to you to put himself in difficulties to let you get by. It is a matter of courtesy, generally, and the skipper of a slower boat should not hog the channel but should invite faster craft to overtake by beckoning them on as soon as he knows that conditions permit a safe overtaking.

On narrow canals, pleasure craft will travel much faster than laden working boats, but the greatest caution should be exercised before attempting to pass. If you come up behind a pair of narrow boats *never* attempt to get past them without being invited to do so by the narrow boat skipper. Stay patiently behind until he waves you on and indicates which side you can safely pass him. Once he has invited you to overtake (and he will probably wait until a suitable deep straight length) he will probably shut down his engine while you go by. Press on then, but take care not to go so hard that your wash spills over his low sides into his cargo. If you try to force past without his approval he will keep going hard, and though you will be faster than he is you will find to your horror that you cannot get past him but will be sucked in alongside him by the effect of disturbed water in a narrow channel. This is very embarrassing for you, and possibly dangerous, and very gratifying for the barge skipper, though his face will not betray a flicker of emotion.

'SOMETHING ROUND THE PROP'

This chapter would not be complete without a look at a few

hazards of inland navigation, and a few words on how to cope with them.

Probably the trouble most commonly encountered on canals, and to a lesser extent on rivers, is getting something caught in the propeller. Most commonly the trouble is caused by weed, but other possibilities include rope, plastic sheet or fertiliser bags, cycle and motor tyres, barbed wire and mattresses. These are listed in ascending order of difficulty.

The first sign of something round the propeller may be engine labouring, sudden vibration or rumbling noise, or simply loss of efficiency so that although the engine speed doesn't seem to alter, the boat goes much more slowly. Steering may also be affected.

Sometimes the trouble can be cured by moving the gear from ahead to astern a few times. This reversing of the prop, one way and then the other, will often shake the clogging material free with no further action.

If this fails, the engine must be stopped and the trouble tackled more directly. Most canal cruisers have weed hatches which, when opened from inside the boat, enable you to reach down to the propeller. The engine must be stopped during the operation for safety— not just put into neutral. It is best to remove the ignition key if possible to guard against anyone pushing the starter in error.

One of the handiest tools for cutting weed or rope off a propeller is a saw bread knife, and most boats have one of these on board. Tougher items like tyres, wire or mattresses will need more sophisticated tools like hacksaws and wire croppers and these are unlikely to be available on a hire cruiser. Help should therefore be sought from the boatyard. The prudent private owner will carry such tools. When using any tool through a weed hatch, it is best to secure it on the end of a length of cord as it is very easy to drop a tool when working under water with cold hands. When the job is complete, don't throw the offending material back in the canal to catch someone else— throw it well clear of the waterway, or keep it for safe disposal later. And do remember to check that the weed hatch is securely fastened after you have started cruising: more than one cruiser has been sunk through neglect of this precaution.

If the boat does not have a weed hatch the problem of clearing the propeller can be more difficult. Reaching underneath with the hook of a boathook is all that is possible from dry land, preferably from a bridgehole where you can bring the boat alongside (but get someone to watch for approaching traffic). If this fails you can try lying on the towpath and reaching below the stern with a bare arm, but the chances are you will have to get into swimming shorts and get right into the water.

With an outboard motor, of course, there is no difficulty, since the whole engine can be tilted clear of the water and the offending material removed at leisure.

Sometimes a propeller can become so badly tangled in really tough material that the boat must be slipped, docked or lifted for a professional attack on the problem, but this is very rare, and perseverance will usually win through in the end. One technique, strictly for experts and *never* for hirers, is to lower the boat gently on to a lock sill as a makeshift means of dry docking the stern end. But this is only possible if the construction of the boat suits the process, and could result in much worse trouble if not properly carried out.

GOING AGROUND

On most inland waterways the deepest part, and therefore the navigable channel, tends to run up the centre on straight lengths and towards the outside of bends. On rivers the scouring action of the current deepens the outside of the bend and deposits mud and gravel on the inside. On canals, barges and narrow boats tend to swing wide round bends to make them as easy as possible to negotiate and their passage keeps the channel open. Therefore never cut corners or you risk going aground. This is a fairly common hazard, though you will do this less as with experience you come to know almost by instinct where the water is shallow and where deep.

When you feel a boat beginning to go aground, go astern immediately. With luck, particularly if you were not going too fast, this will pull you off again. Rocking the boat from side to side will often help to free it from mud, while the engine is kept astern. But you must be cautious in the use of the engine if you are aground on a hard bottom: there is a risk of damaging the propeller. The least grinding or banging sound from astern is your warning here, and you should shut down immediately.

If the bottom is hard, you will probably be able to push off with a boathook or even get over the side and shove off by a direct push. If the water is shallow enough to ground you you can be certain you are in no danger of drowning.

If the boat is aground at the bows don't all rush up forward during attempts to refloat. Move everyone possible right down aft, leaving just one person forward to push off. This alteration in trim is often enough to achieve the desired result on a hard bottom, but not in mud. (Remember this technique if you ever knock a hole in the boat on or below the water-line. Don't let all your crew rush to the damaged point. Get them to the other side, so that their weight will lift the damage above the water.)

The trouble with mud is that your boathook will sink in when you try to push off and you will have a struggle to pull it free again. In addition to rocking the boat, try using the boathook at the other end to swing the boat from side to side, while going astern with the engine.

If all these methods fail, tie all your ropes together and get them across to the bank. If there are no passers-by to give you a pull, you and the crew will have to swim or wade ashore and do the heaving yourself. Always pull back in the line which the boat took when she went aground. Of course, if a passing boat comes along you can ask them for a 'snatch'—the traditional canal method of getting free of mud. In this the tug takes your rope and makes it fast, then backs up to get some slack. It then goes hard ahead gathering way until the tow-rope suddenly tightens. This produces a real heave on the line and, repeated if necessary several times, will pull any boat off any mud-bank.

WIND

High wind is another navigational hazard on inland waters and the best advice to beginners is to tie up until it moderates. If you must proceed you will need full power and will have to proceed crabwise. The danger of this procedure is that if you do get blown aground or into the bank, your engine will be going at full speed and the risk of damage is high. The wind nearly always moderates towards evening, so it is best to moor up and wait. If yours is a fairly heavy boat, and the wind is blowing off the towpath side, a member of the crew walking along the path with a line to the bow can keep her straight.

TOWING FROM THE BANK

It sometimes happens that you have to tow your boat from the towpath—perhaps as a result of engine failure, propeller or rudder damage or even running out of fuel. This is not hard work and even a child can pull a large cruiser easily. (This is why water transport is economical: small power units can move large loads.) But there are a couple of tricks worth knowing. First of all, you need a long, light rope—the longer the better, so that the pull can be as near as possible in line with the direction you want to take. If you don't carry a long line, join all the mooring ropes together and add the clothes-line as well. Second, don't fasten the tow-rope to the bow cleat in the middle of the foredeck, but attach it to the side of the boat about a third of the way back from the bow. If there isn't a mooring cleat at this point attach to a fender eye or handrail, or take the line in through a cabin window and secure the end somewhere suitable. You will then find

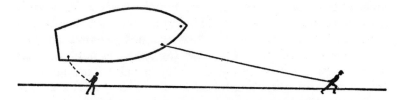

FIG 2   Correct method of towing a boat from the bank in the case of engine failure. Use a *long* rope made fast about one-third of the boat's length from the bows. A second rope from the stern and a second 'horse' will be necessary if the steering does not work

that the boat will swim along sweetly, and not keep nosing into the bank. If your rudder still works she will steer easily. If it doesn't you will need another line from the stern to the towpath and a person on each rope. These two ropes will enable steering to be achieved while towing: if the stern man pulls in the bow will swing away from the towpath; if the bow man wants the boat to head towards him he has only to shorten his rope and pull the head towards him. In this way you can cover the miles quite effortlessly, making for help.

ACCIDENTS

We should now briefly look at the correct procedure in the event of an accident, even at the risk of giving the impression that inland cruising is an endlessly perilous business. If you are involved in an accident with another vessel, proceed as you would in a road accident. Get the other skipper's name and address, the name of his boat and, if possible the name of his insurance company. Give him the same information about yourself. If either vessel is a hire cruiser the owners should be informed as soon as possible and given all the information. If the boat is your own, advise your own insurers of the details as soon as possible. If the damage is not such as to prevent you from cruising, get the boat into the hands of competent repairers as soon as possible and they will assist you in sorting out the repairs with the insurance company. Remember that your insurers will always support you in any prudent action you take to mitigate a disaster: in other words if you are leaking badly do not defer getting assistance until you have been able to contact your insurers. Do the best you can to prevent the situation becoming worse, and if you have to hire help or incur expense in doing so you will always be covered.

If the worst comes to the worst and you are sinking with no help at hand, try to run the boat into shallow water and get as much of your personal effects and the boat's loose gear ashore as possible. If the engine is an outboard get this off if time permits. Moor up firmly with extra ropes. On inland waters you are unlikely to sink very far and a cool head can reduce the damage very considerably.

While looking at disasters, we'll mention two more matters where very special care is essential, and then we can return to the more normal matters of navigation. The two dangerous commodities carried aboard most craft are fuel and bottled gas. Petrol is more dangerous than diesel but diesel oil will burn dramatically if a boat does catch fire. Therefore always take special care to ensure that no naked flames or cigarettes are about when you are tipping fuel into your tank, and take care to ensure that spare petrol cans are safely stowed, upright and with caps securely closed. Keep your petrol tank, tubing, filters and engine constantly in good order to guard against leaks, and ensure that all electrical circuits are safe and not prone to sparks or shorting. Similarly with bottled gas: make sure the installation is a good one, with the cylinders either on deck or, if inboard, in a metal lined locker ventilated outboard. Gas tubing should be copper with proper fittings—not rubber hose—and all tubing should be exposed and accessible, not hidden behind panelling or under floors. Don't leave saucepans and kettle unattended: if they boil over they can extinguish the flame and allow gas to escape. Bottled gas is heavier than air and will sink to the bilges if it escapes in the boat. If you find that gas *has* escaped, stop engine, put out all flames, stop smoking, and open all windows and doors. Then take up all floorboards and thoroughly ventilate the whole boat. If you swing floorboards gently back and forth you will stir up the gas by causing air turbulence, and a good draught through the cabin will soon dissipate it. (If you are on a hired boat, *always* report a serious gas escape to the boatyard. Do not try to deal with it unaided.) Finally, make sure you carry at least one good suitable fire extinguisher and that all crew members know how to use it; preferably dry powder, which is safe for all types of fire and non-toxic.

TURNING THE BOAT

With this glance, in passing, at the possible misfortunes that can happen, we can return to the business of cruising. Only two points of normal cruising remain to be covered: turning round in a narrow channel, and mooring up. In turning a boat always remember that the deepest and most vulnerable part of the craft is right aft where the propeller and rudder are located. Therefore, although you can nose the bow right into a bank when turning, the stern must be kept in deep water. In a narrow channel attempting to turn as you would turn a car in a narrow road, by going ahead and astern, is not to be recommended for fear of going too far astern. The safest way to turn if you are in any doubt is to come alongside and turn the boat by hand, using ropes and boathook. If you are a little more expert, another method is to steer the bow very slowly and gently in to the bank, so that it rests against a bit of soft grass and not rocks or stones. If you then keep the engine in ahead gear slowly, with the wheel hard over, the boat will slowly pivot round its nose. At the last moment, when it is almost round and before the stern comes into shallow water, you can back off into the channel and start forward again.

MOORING UP

The same cautionary note applies to mooring up—watch out for your propeller and rudder if the water is shallow. On canals with no current to worry about you simply moor alongside in the direction you are heading. On rivers you must first swing round if you are travelling downstream so that you come into your moorings against the current.

On canals, moorings will almost always be on the towpath side.

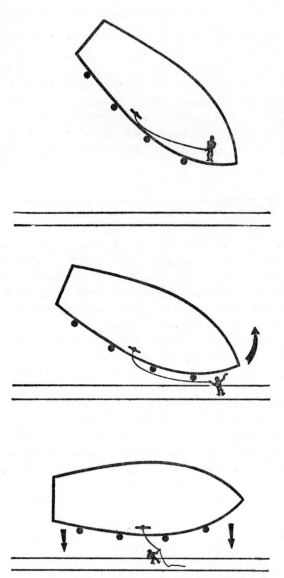

FIG 3 The use of a centre rope greatly simplifies coming alongside
quickly and is particularly useful when there is only one crew member
available or an offshore wind. The top illustration shows boat approaching bank, fenders down, and with crewman at bow holding end of
centre rope. As the bow reaches the bank (*centre picture*) the crewman
steps ashore, turns and pushes the bow off to prevent it from bumping.
This puts the boat parallel to the bank, a few feet out (*bottom picture*)
and a pull on the centre line is all that is needed to bring it alongside.

Choose a spot with a good firm bank or concrete wall, well clear of bridges and bends, and where the waterway is wide enough for traffic to pass you easily when you are moored. Regular mooring places are listed in the Inland Cruising Booklets (see Chapter 10), but you are not limited to these. Put your fenders out and approach with caution, taking your boat out of gear and drifting the last few feet. Mooring up will be made much easier by the use of a centre rope. This is a rope fixed to a cleat on the deck amidships on the side

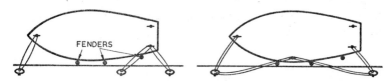

FENDERS

FIG 4   Two methods of mooring a small cruiser using 'springs' to prevent the boat surging back and forth in the wash of passing craft. In the left-hand example, three rings or stakes in the bank are needed; on the right two rings are used and separate fore and aft ropes (called springs) are made fast to the midships cleat on the boat. (If the boat hasn't a midships cleat the spring from the stern cleat would go to the forward ring and vice versa)

nearest the bank. A member of the crew, holding the loose end of this rope, will stand up in the bow as you edge towards the bank. As soon as you are near enough, he can jump ashore and push the bow off, so that the boat will be lying parallel to the bank a few feet out. By pulling on the centre rope he can then pull the whole boat bodily

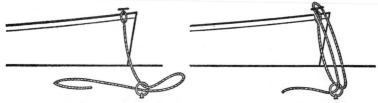

FIG 5   The two illustrations above show a quick method of making fast to a ring when using a long line. First, pull a loop of rope through the ring—don't thread the whole line laboriously through. Next, pull the loop so that it is large enough to be taken back to the cleat and dropped over it. The loose end can be either tied off at the ring or, if long enough, taken back and made fast to the cleat. This makes a strong mooring that won't let you break adrift. The same technique can be used with a bollard or stake

sideways in to the bank, which is much easier than trying to get two people ashore at the same time, one with the bow rope and one with the stern rope. Once you are alongside, of course, bow and stern lines should be got out and the boat moored properly fore and aft with these.

At regular mooring points you will probably find mooring rings or bollards to make fast to. In the wilds you will need to use your own mooring stakes. These should be driven well down, angled away from the boat so that the lines can't slip off. Stakes should be driven between the towpath and the water, so that mooring lines are not stretched across the path.

TRAILING

Many motorists enjoy taking a trailed craft with them on an outing or a holiday. This can give a lot of fun, but please remember:

(a) to observe the speed limit of the water you are on;
(b) to obtain a licence in advance. Otherwise to pay the boatyard where you launch (if they are empowered to collect fees), or the nearest waterway official. Navigation authorities can and do proceed against the owners of unlicensed boats.
(c) to take care not to butt into races or competitions organised by boat clubs, or into stretches of water set aside for the special activities of certain clubs, as certain stretches of the Trent are by agreement reserved for the Trent Power Boat and Ski Club on certain days.

7 (*Above*) Grand Union Canal scene near Hemel Hempstead: locks, swing bridge and waterside pub beneath the gentle slope of the Chilterns; (*below*) tip-up drawbridge, typical of many such on the southern section of the Oxford Canal. They can be awkward on a windy day.

8 (*Above*) An inland marina: pleasure
craft mooring centre at Braunston near
Rugby. Such inland 'harbours' may soon
become a common sight on amenity
waterways; (*below*) mixed bag of inland
craft on the Great Ouse at St Ives in
Huntingdonshire: converted ship's life-
boat, motor cruiser and sailing cruiser.

CHAPTER FIVE

Bridges, Tunnels and Locks

The various types of bridge, the occasional tunnels you will pass through, the locks you will meet, offer you no real difficulties. But, because novices are sometimes worried by what they anticipate but have not yet experienced, we have written this explanatory chapter.

BLIND CORNERS AND BRIDGEHOLES

Some bends are so sharp that you cannot see round them, and often a bridge will obscure the view still further. In such circumstances proceed with caution and give a long steady blast on your hooter. (You *must* have a hooter to comply with waterway by-laws and for your own safety.) If your hooter is a car-type electric horn, don't blow a couple of short parps, which could be mistaken for a car crossing the road bridge, but a long steady blast for a count of ten or more. Listen carefully for an answer and repeat. It is a good idea to have a crew member up forward as a look-out and listen-out. Being away from the engine noise he is more likely to hear a reply than the helmsman. If there is no reply, go ahead steadily but on the alert for evasive action. If there is a reply, and you can't judge whether you or the unknown oncoming boat will reach the blind bridge first, play it safe and hang back until he appears. There is no more alarming sight than the sudden appearance of the high steel bows of an oncoming barge or narrow boat in a blind bridge-hole, and none more certain to cause panic in a novice-skipper's heart. If you can't see clearly ahead, remember that you can't just stop dead all at once if you see something —so go slowly.

People have a nasty habit of dropping things into the canal on each side of bridges, especially those in towns or villages. There may be bricks, or coping stones off the parapet, or unwanted sacks or clothes. So slow down for these, which brings your propeller up, or even

E 73

coast through in neutral if you think fit, which reduces the chances of picking up something.

SWING AND LIFT BRIDGES

Minor roads and farm tracks are often carried across the canal on movable bridges. These may be pivoted, and swing, being moved either by pushing the land end round, or by a windlass and chain; or they may lift. Lifting bridges are worked by someone pulling down the counterbalancing beam with a chain or a boathook to raise the roadway.

Such bridges are unmanned except on the busiest waterways. Where they are manned, all that is required is a long blast on the hooter to announce your approach and in due course the bridge will open to permit your passage. When you have to operate them yourself, the procedure is quite simple. If you have a large crew, of course, the simplest thing is to put a couple of people ashore before the bridge and let them go ahead and open it while you proceed slowly through. If you are short-handed you may have to come into the bank before the bridge and go ahead and open it yourself, returning to navigate the boat through. You will have to moor again, of course, to return and close the bridge. The actual type of bridge can vary widely, but the method of operation is usually simply apparent. On the southern section of the Oxford Canal there are many tip-up bridges and some of these can be awkward. Where the bridge is not provided with any kind of catch to secure it in the up position it is best to leave the crew member involved to sit on the balance beam while someone else navigates the boat through. Some of these bridges are quite delicately balanced, and a gust of wind can bring them crashing down if they are not firmly secured or sat on. It is inadvisable to let a child do the operating: give the job to an adult.

Always leave a bridge as you found it.

AQUEDUCTS

An aqueduct carries the canal over a road, river, or railway. Navigating it needs no special technique; simply, in some cases, a good head for heights and perhaps a moment to reflect that the early canal engineers who built them probably carried out no complicated calculations. They just built them, and there they still are, unlikely now to collapse as you steam over, whatever secret horrors you may be entertaining.

If it is an iron trough aqueduct, with a path on one side only, put children in the cabin or in the cockpit with you, or let them run along the towpath, but don't have them on the cabin roof, or where you can't see what they are doing.

TUNNELS

Tunnels are either wide, with enough room for two narrow craft to pass, or narrow, in which case traffic has to be regulated to one-way only either by a tunnel-keeper, signals or hours restriction. Narrow tunnels have either a tunnel-keeper to instruct you or clearly displayed information. In narrow tunnels there is very little room to spare and all you can do is to try as best you can to keep from scraping the sides. In wide tunnels the problem is not so acute and you can steer down the middle without difficulty, slowing down and getting over to the right side only if you meet oncoming craft. It is pitch dark in a canal tunnel—the daylight fades a very short distance from the entrance—so you essentially need a good, bright headlight. If your boat has red and green navigation lights, use these as well. They will identify you as a pleasure boat to oncoming barges. A useful trick, even on a dull day, is to wear dark glasses for the last ten minutes or so before entering a tunnel, removing them only when you are in the gloom. This will accustom your eyes to the dark and you will see much more easily.

Tunnels, though perhaps a little alarming even to the experienced skipper if he has any imagination, are fascinating to navigate. The bricks or stonework is often quite black overhead, recalling the old steamboats and tugs, and long stalactites will hang from the roof, the result of water seeping through the lime mortar. Often there are vertical air shafts at intervals, casting a circle of ghostly light on the water, and sometimes from these shafts cascades of cold spring water descend on the passing navigators. Some tunnels have distance plaques along the walls, to encourage the leggers who worked the boats through before the days of power. The air temperature inside the tunnels hardly varies from winter to summer, so that they seem warm in winter and cool in summer. Sometimes this temperature contrast can cause localised mist to form just inside the entrance but this only persists for a few yards. In the old days, when many commercial craft used the canals, tunnels could be almost choked with the exhaust fumes from diesel engines and smoke from cabin chimneys, so that it was quite impossible to see through them and the daylight from the distant exit only showed up a matter of a minute or so before you emerged. Nowadays, with the falling off in narrow boat traffic, the tunnels are usually clear and the far end can be seen as a bright point of light almost as soon as you enter.

LOCKS

Locks, like tunnels, tend to alarm the beginner before he has had any experience of them and then, after he has mastered the simple procedures involved, he wonders what on earth he was worried about. There are no locks on the Broads, of course, but plenty of them on canals and rivers. Locks on rivers like the Thames, Severn, Trent and on certain heavily used commercial canals are manned, that is to say, attended and operated by lock-keepers, and may be mechanically operated, whereas the majority of locks on the narrow canal system and on rivers with little or no commercial traffic are unmanned and must be hand-operated by the boatman. Some canals do have so-called lock-keepers, who will often be in charge of a whole flight of locks rather than just a single unit, but their job is to keep an eye on the operation of the flight, and make sure that passing craft operate the gates and paddles properly, rather than to work the locks for you, or assist you in working them. If they do, this is a courtesy rather than a duty, and should be treated as such.

When passing through manned locks, on the Thames for example, the skipper is not involved in any responsibility for the actual operation of the lock machinery, and is free to concentrate on looking after his boat. During the busy cruising season, Thames locks are in operation all day long with craft passing up and down. It is simply a matter of waiting your turn, usually in company with other craft, to enter the lock chamber once emerging craft have left it. At quieter times, however, you may come round a corner to see that the lock is not in use and with no lock-keeper in sight. A long blast on your hooter will notify the keeper of your approach, and as you steam towards the lock you will see his white-capped figure emerge. If the lock is ready for you, you can steam straight in, make fast alongside and shut off the engine. The lock-keeper will then close the gates behind you and work the sluices to raise or lower you as the case may be. If you are ascending you will need to take your ropes in as the boat rises and they slacken, and to keep an eye open to ensure that the rising boat does not catch under any overhanging projection. If you are descending it is, of course, even more important to ensure that someone is watching and slackening the ropes as the boat descends. Failure to keep an eye on this can have one of three results: the ropes will break; the deck cleats will break or rip off; or, if ropes are strong and cleats solidly fixed, the whole boat will be hung up in the air. The best method when descending is to pass the mooring rope round a lockside bollard and bring it back on board, holding on to the end, without making fast. Then you can pay out as the boat falls.

Often the lock chambers on Thames locks are packed solid with craft during the busy season, so that your crew must also ensure that your boat is not fouling another. Enter and leave locks carefully always, especially when other craft are already in the chamber. And remember that you may be the skipper of your boat but the lock-keeper is the boss during locking operations and you must do as he says. (Thames keepers are all retired seafaring men so don't try to tell them anything about boating.)

Since you will get plenty of help and advice from these friendly and experienced men, there is no point here in going into more detail about passing through manned locks. Work a few under their watchful eye and you will learn more than from whole chapters of theory.

On the canals and on rivers where the locks are not manned it is different, however. There you are on your own, responsible not only for the safe passage of your own boat but also for leaving the lock correctly set for the next user. So you must have a fairly clear idea in your head of what is involved before you start messing about with the gear.

All locks, regardless of what machinery they may use to achieve it, work on the same principle which is simplicity itself: they let water in from one end to raise the level, or they let it out at the other end to lower it. The lock itself is simply two parallel walls with gates of one kind or another at each end. It may be 'broad', wide enough to take two 7 ft narrow boats side by side, or 'narrow', just wide enough for one. The only mistake of any consequence that you can make in operating a lock is to let the water run straight through it at both ends, so that it neither fills or empties but merely wastes water to no avail. Water is let into the lock at the top end through sluices (called paddles on most canals, cloughs pronounced 'clows', in the north) and out

77

again at the bottom end through further sluices. Obviously, if you are filling the lock at the top end you must ensure that the sluices at the bottom end are first closed. And vice versa. And that's really all there is to it. Dramatic mistakes, such as beginners envisage, involving opening the wrong gates and allowing a tidal wave of water to engulf the boat and the low-lying countryside for miles around, simply are not possible. You *can't* open a lock gate too soon: the water pressure against it is too great to permit it to be moved until the level both sides has equalised, when it will open sweetly in response to a steady push on the balance beam.

The paddles themselves may be operated by a variety of tackle and may be situated in the gates themselves or on the ground beside the lock. Don't let them awe you: they are no more than a wooden shutter which blocks a hole to prevent water passing through when they are down (ie closed) or opens the hole to allow water to pass through when you wind them up. Some have fixed winding handles, or wheels, by which they are operated: most, however, are worked by a cranked spanner—called a windlass (sometimes a key)—which the boatman owns and carries with him. This has a square tapered hole in one end and this hole fits over a square tapered spindle on the gear. Cranking the windlass operates a rack and pinion mechanism to raise or lower the paddle down below. Normally, as the paddle itself lifts up, so does a paddle-bar rise above the pinion. There is usually some form of ratchet or other device by which the paddle can be locked in the raised position.

The gates at each end are usually simply large wooden 'doors' and on most locks there are two of these at each end which meet in a V pointing upstream, or towards the higher level, so that the water pressure forces them tightly together to prevent them leaking. On narrow canals the double V gates sometimes appear only at the lower end of the lock, with a single flat gate at the upper end which swings through a complete right-angle and closes the top of the lock like a dam straight across it. Occasionally, you will find narrow locks with single doors at both top and bottom.

Whether single or double, all these are simply varieties of the traditional and familiar lock gate and they are opened and closed much like a common house door, except that instead of being on hinges they are pivoted on a vertical heel-post. Usually the top member of the gate is extended over the land to form a balance beam, the gate being opened and shut by pushing on the end of this. A balance beam

78

does, in fact, balance the gate so that the weight on the heel-post is minimised and the gate can be swung easily.

There is, however, another type of gate for closing the ends of locks, the guillotine gate. This is raised and lowered vertically, and a considerable structure is required to achieve this, since there have to be balance weights to ease the effort required in operation, and the whole gate must in any case be raised sufficiently high into the air to allow the boat to pass beneath it when entering and leaving the lock. This type of gate is rare on the canals, although there are two narrow locks in operation using this system, at Kings Norton where the Stratford-upon-Avon canal joins the Worcester & Birmingham, and at Thurlwood on the Trent & Mersey. On the beautiful River Nene—from Northampton to Peterborough and beyond—all the locks make use of guillotines at the lower end, though they have normal wooden V-gates (called 'pointing doors' by the River Authority) at the upper end. Two of the Nene locks make use of still further a variation, as do some Great Ouse locks. Instead of having vertical guillotines they have radial guillotines—which work on a curve instead of straight up and down. Usually there are no sluices or paddles on guillotine gates, since water can be passed by simply raising the gate an inch or so to allow the water to flow under it. Unfortunately, the River Authority require the locks to be left with the guillotine raised and the wooden upper gates closed, so that navigating the river in either direction always involves working each lock twice—tiring exercise since some ninety turns are required on the guillotine windlass to raise or lower the gate. (In passing it should be noted that the effort is well worth it: the river is delightful particularly in its lower reaches, quite unspoiled and all its navigational gear is always in first-class condition.)

Now let's look at the problem of working a boat through a lock, assuming a minimum crew of skipper and mate. The procedure will be the same whether it is a wide lock or a narrow one, with double V-gates or single door at each end. We will assume in the first instance that you are descending and later will look at the problems involved in travelling the other way and ascending.

As you approach the lock it will be either 'ready' for you or 'against' you, and you will be able to see which from quite a distance. (Field glasses are very useful here.) The lock is said to be ready for you if the gates at your end are open and you can sail straight in. Assume it is ready and proceed into the chamber. As the lock is a full one—remember you are about to descend—your boat will be well above the locksides, and you can come alongside normally, coming to a stop for preference about the middle of the lock and well clear of the gates at both ends. Stop engine and both crew members disembark, one taking the lock windlass and the other holding the mooring lines to keep the boat in position. The other crew member then goes back to close the gates through which you have just entered. If it is a wide lock you will have to close one gate and then go round to the other side of the lock (across the gates at the other end if there isn't a footbridge) to close the gate on the far side. If it is a narrow lock the chances are that there will be just the single gate to close and you will, of course, have moored up on the heel-post side, which is always to the towpath.

Having closed the gate or gates behind you, next check that the sluices at this end of the lock are lowered and shut. Since you found the lock ready for you the implication is that the last boat through was coming up (you will have met him earlier) and he will have had to open these top sluices to fill the lock. He may or may not have closed them, so you must check them and close them if necessary. (You simply wind them down with your windlass, lifting the safety ratchet clear to allow you to do so.) If the paddle-bar is up, the paddle is open. So see it is right down, and the paddle fully closed.

The boat is now in a full lock, with all gates closed and all sluices closed. Nothing happening. The next step therefore is to walk to the lower end of the lock and open the sluices to let the water out. Open them steadily, one after the other, making sure the safety ratchet is in place to hold them open before you let go of your windlass.

Danger warning here: NEVER, NEVER let go of your windlass when it is on a paddle: always take it off and keep it in your hand. If the ratchet should fail with your windlass in position it will whirl it round viciously until it suddenly flies off. If it hits you it will probably injure you badly. If it misses you it will probably fly into the canal leaving you stuck.

With the lower sluices open, the water will start to empty from the lock chamber. There will be a great turbulence down below the lock where the sluices gush out into the canal, but none in the lock. The water will fall smoothly and silently, and the crew member on the ropes will pay out enough slack to allow the boat to descend. The boat may have a tendency to move towards the lower gates as the lock empties, but this will be only gentle. It won't matter if it does approach them, but is better kept away in case the bow catches on the gates and gets hung up.

As the water level falls it will uncover and expose to your view the biggest danger involved in going down in a lock. This is the sill against which the upper gates close—a wide shelf of masonry at the foot of the upper gates which is not visible when the lock is full. If you allow your boat to stay too near the top gates as the lock empties the stern of your boat may catch on this, and your vital parts—rudder and propeller—are right at the back and subject to damage. This is why, on entering the lock, you went half-way along the chamber and tied up about the middle. A smallish cruiser should never foul a lock sill, but a 70 ft narrow boat has only a couple of feet to spare and must be kept with its bow hard against the bottom gates while the lock empties. If two cruisers lock through together to save time and water, then the first should be well forward to give the second plenty of room to clear the sill.

When the lock is quite empty, the gate man can push open the lower gates and you are clear to proceed. If the lock was not a very deep one, the man holding the ropes will have been able to get back on board just as the lock was nearly empty and will have the ropes stowed and the engine running as the gates are opened. He can then take the boat gently out, picking up the gate man from the lower level as the boat emerges from the chamber, or, if there is any difficulty about this, from the bank lower down, or the first bridge-hole. If the lock was very deep, or the crew member not able easily to scramble down while the boat is in the lock, he can simply tow it out of the lock with the ropes and both can climb aboard from the lower level.

It is a courtesy to the next lock user to drop the paddles again once the gates are open, but it is not necessary to close the gates behind you. You leave the lock 'ready' for an ascending boat.

This is all that is involved in locking down and we can summarise the procedure as follows:

1 Enter the lock, proceed half-way along and disembark, with mooring ropes, on towpath side.
2 Close gates behind you and ensure sluices also closed.
3 Proceed to lower end of lock with windlass and open sluices to let water out. Pay out ropes as water falls.
4 Open lower gates when lock empty and close sluices as courtesy measure. If you can get on board again in lock do so and

motor out and away. If too deep to board in lock, pull boat clear of chamber with ropes and reboard below lock.

You will recall that in this example we assumed that the lock was ready for you and you were able to cruise straight in. If you had found that the lock was 'against' you as you approached it you would not have been able to sail in because the gates nearest you would have been closed. You would therefore come into the towpath a short distance away from the lock, moor the boat up or leave someone looking after it, and proceed to make the lock ready for you. This would involve closing the lower gates and lowering sluices, raising the top sluices to fill the lock, and opening the top gates to admit your own boat. Thereafter, the procedure would be as just described. It is important to keep the boat a little distance from the lock during this filling operation, and to have it held securely. This is because there will be quite a strong current in the narrow entry to the lock when the water is rushing into the chamber to fill it. This can suck the boat towards the gates with great force.

It is worth remembering that if you meet a boat as you approach a lock, he will have left it ready for you. If you are following behind a boat he will leave the locks against you. Where possible, pleasure craft travelling in the same direction should share locks to save water, and if you know there is another cruiser close behind as you approach a lock you should wait to share it with him. This will pay you, in any case, because there will be extra hands to work the gates and paddles and your time through the locks will therefore be reduced. This is particularly useful if you are tackling a flight of locks which are all against you, since the extra people available will allow for one or more to go ahead getting the next lock ready.

Now we must look at the problems involved in locking uphill. If this seems an awful lot of words about locks, and an alarming series of do's and don'ts, you may take comfort from the fact that it really is all very simple when you actually come to do it.

Once again, we'll start by assuming that the lock is ready for you and that you could steam straight into the chamber if you wished. However, the lock sides from this approach will be high above you and if it happens to be a deep lock you may find difficulty in scrambling up once the boat is in the chamber. If it is deep, the best thing is to come alongside the towpath below the lock, get the mooring lines and the windlass ashore, and stop the engine. You can then tow the boat into the chamber, once again stopping midway along the lock.

Again, one man holds the ropes while the other closes the gates through which you have just entered and checks that the sluices are all closed.

He then proceeds to the top of the lock and works the sluices to let the water in to fill it. Caution is needed here, since the water is now rushing into the lock and the turbulence which was outside and below the lock during the downhill operation will now be inside the chamber as the water rushes in from the upper level.

You will notice that on most locks there are paddles in the upper gates themselves, which admit water through them, and also paddles on the sides of the lock and ahead of it, which let water into the lock below the surface through tunnels that run round the gates. The correct procedure is first to open the ground paddles only, half-way to begin with, thus reducing the initial turbulence, and then fully. When the lock is about half-full, open first one gate paddle and then the other. It is, incidentally, a golden rule that those working the paddles should always watch the boat while doing it, so that they can at once close them again if the water is entering too violently. The rope man will have more to do as the turbulence will tend to draw the boat back and forth, but provided he doesn't let it creep forward into the area of broken water, and keeps the boat towards the middle or lower end where the water is calmer, this will not present any problems. The turbulence in any case rapidly abates as the level rises and it is only during the first minute or so that it can be violent, particularly if the sluices are fully drawn.

The rope man must watch to ensure that the rising boat does not become jammed under any projections in the lock side. On old locks the masonry is sometimes in poor condition, with bricks projecting or hollows where some brickwork has fallen away. The edge of the deck or a rubbing strake can sometimes catch in these and if this is not spotted the boat can be damaged.

If a boat catches and jams in a lock either ascending or descending, do not waste time trying to free it by pushing or pulling. Immediately close the paddles to stop the water flow, and run smartly to the other end of the lock and open a paddle there. This will reverse the flow and the boat will soon come free.

Once the lock is full, the top gates can be opened and top sluices closed, the crew can easily reboard the boat and you can sail away.

SPECIAL NOTE: On most canals with wide locks it is customary to leave the locks with the gates open after ascending. On narrow canals, particularly those which have locks with double V-gates at the bottom and a single gate at the top, it is usually necessary to close this top gate behind you when you leave a full lock, since this single gate is designed to be fully water-tight. The double gates at the lower end of narrow locks often leak badly and if the top gate were not shut a great deal of water could escape. All sluices should be closed when you leave any lock.

Once again, a brief summary:

1 Approach lock and if sides are not too high sail straight in. If sides too high to allow for getting off, stop below lock and pull boat into chamber with ropes. Stay towards middle or lower end.
2 Close gates and paddles behind you.
3 Open top sluices carefully to avoid turbulence, first the ground paddles, then those on the gate.
4 When lock full, open top gate, close sluices and motor away. (If narrow lock, close top gate behind you when boat is out.) As you leave, look back and see all paddle-bars are down, meaning all sluices closed.

Of course, if you find the lock against you you must tie up below, and go ahead to empty it before you can get in. It is very important to tie at least 50 yards clear of the lock during this process, for the emerging water causes much turbulence below the lock. This applies equally if a boat is in the lock coming down. You would expect this water to blow your boat back clear of the gates if by mistake you moored too close. In fact, because the sluices come out well below water level, the current is violently away from the lock at the bottom of the canal, while the surface water (in which you float) rushes violently *towards* the gates. This can swiftly suck your boat forward into the gates with a great crash, which is bad enough, but there is a further danger. The force of the water emerging tends to blow the water away from the tail of the lock, so that the level drops briefly but appreciably. If your boat nose-dives forward while the level is briefly lowered, and the bow dives under one of the great oak cross members of the lock gate, the returning water level will force the bow up violently under this beam and damage will result before you get clear. So keep well back from below locks when emptying them.

There is one small difficulty to watch for when approaching a lock going uphill. At one side you will usually find a stream of water entering the canal, the overflow from the pound above. This will tend to push your boat sideways as you are trying to enter the lock, with a final tendency to move the stern away from the stream, and the bow towards it. Therefore approach the lock a little on the stream side of the entrance—not too much—and, if you've judged it correctly, the stream will straighten you up to enter the lock. But they don't all come in at the same angle, and you may not get it right. If you do hit the side wall of the lock a little harder than you meant to, others have done it before you.

There are varieties of locks, of course, and staircases where one chamber leads into another and the water is discharged into and drawn from side lagoons. To attempt an explanation of all varieties here would only be confusing and daunting. Local advice is always available where locks present special complexities so these need not here concern the general reader. You will find detailed information in the Inland Cruising Booklets.

Similarly, on some canals, locks are provided with side ponds as a means of economising in the use of water. Generally these are only employed in times of drought or impending drought and waterways staff will then be in evidence to ensure their use. Since they are perfectly simple a brief word of explanation may be in order here. A side pond is a chamber beside the lock, connected to it by an additional sluice. Sometimes there are two of these at different levels. On entering a lock to descend, having closed all gates, the boatman raises the paddle between the lock and the upper pond, letting the lock drain into this pond until the levels equate. He then closes the paddle trapping a pond full of water. He next opens the paddle connecting the lock with the lower pond and repeats, trapping a second pondful. Finally, he opens the lower sluices in the ordinary way, allowing the remaining water in the lock to empty away into the lower level of canal and eventually to waste over a weir somewhere. When an ascending boat enters the lock and closes the gates he opens the paddle from the lower pond and allows this to drain into the lock. When this lower pond is empty, the paddle is closed and the upper pond is similarly emptied into the lock. Finally, the water required to complete the filling is drawn from the upper level in the normal way. Double side ponds like this can save two-thirds of a lockful of water at each use—and water is the precious raw material of canals.

CHAPTER SIX

Hiring a Boat

H iring a boat for your holiday is the easy way to enjoy the pleasures of boating with none of the worries. You do the cruising—someone else looks after all the chores: the insurance, licensing, cleaning, servicing and maintenance. If you live a long way from water, or are a busy person with little leisure time available for 'week-end' boating and tinkering with boats, then hiring a boat for a holiday cruise has everything to commend it. But, though holiday hiring draws its main stream of customers from those who for one reason or another can never look forward to the pleasures of owning a boat of their own, it also offers to those contemplating the purchase of a boat a comparatively cheap way of finding out just how much they enjoy boating. Many owners of private craft first caught the boating bug (*virus nauticus*—an infection of the head and heart leading to years of happiness) aboard a hired cruiser.

Hiring a boat also offers other advantages. The choice of cruising ground is wide open with no problems of transporting your boat from one area to another. Cruisers of all sizes may be hired in almost every part of the country, on canals, rivers, Broads and lakes; in other countries too, particularly in Ireland, the Netherlands and France. The choice is yours.

Finally, and perhaps most appealing of all, hiring offers you the chance to skipper a much bigger and more luxurious boat than you could probably afford to buy.

Many people believe that only experts can handle boats and, having no experience of boating themselves, are diffident of taking on the responsibility of handling a hired cruiser. There is no need for this diffidence. Cruiser hiring firms demand no proof of experience and welcome beginners. The biggest hire operator on the inland waterways stresses in his advertising that 'novices are welcome' and he, and many others, offers special advance tuition to anyone who is in any doubt. Generally, however, boat hiring firms find that special tuition is quite unnecessary and that the short demonstration run offered to all hirers at the beginning of a cruise is quite sufficient to impart the basic rudiments of boat handling. Practice makes perfect, and hire boats are built to take a fair degree of punishment. Most hire firms, in any case, send useful 'cruising hints' publications to all customers in sufficient time before the cruise to allow for study. Many hire operators frankly *prefer* the complete novice, who is willing to listen and act on advice and instructions from the boatyard, to the 'experienced' hirer who knows it all and sometimes tends to bite off more than he can chew. Lack of experience need deter no one.

Having decided on a holiday on a hired cruiser, there are three basic decisions to make: (1) in what area to cruise; (2) with which firm to book; and (3) which boat to hire. In all three basic decisions, the area of choice will be wider the earlier you book. Inland cruising is extremely popular for holidays nowadays, and the demand outruns the supply of boats, particularly during the height of the season and in school holidays. Many hirers are confirmed addicts and book their next holiday cruise at least a year ahead. If, therefore, you are limited to choice of holiday dates, the sooner you sort out your arrangements the more likely you are to be able to book the boat of your choice for the dates of your holiday. If you are not tied by fixed holiday dates, choose early or late in the year—prices are much lower then than in the season. Avoiding the main holiday period will give you other bonuses besides reduced hire charges: the countryside in spring and autumn has its own particular charms, the waterways are less busy (and therefore truer to their tranquil selves) and you will have more chance to make contact with the regular inhabitants of the waterway world—boatmen, lock-keepers, maintenance men—most of whom are quiet country folk who feel a warmer kinship with the independent out-of-season traveller than with the main rush of high season holiday makers.

Having read Chapter 3, and got some ideas for possible cruises, the next step is to study the advertisements of the various hire cruiser companies offering holiday craft on the water you have decided to explore. These advertisements are usually to be found in the classified sections of the 'quality' Sunday papers, in travel and holiday sections of general magazines and, at all times, in the columns of the boating magazines (see Chapter 10). In addition, lists of hire firms can be obtained from the trade associations and other bodies listed in Chapter 10.

From advertisements and from these lists, it is fairly simple to find which firms offer craft in the area you have decided to explore. Then write to a selected few of them, asking for a copy of their brochure. In writing, be sure that your name and address are clearly legible—print them for preference. Ideally, enclose a sticky self-addressed reply label (*not* a small envelope—most brochures are quite large) and if the advertisement has asked for a small fee for the brochure, enclose this either in postage stamps or by postal order. This request for a small fee sometimes annoys would-be hirers. In fact, it is quite reasonable. Even the simplest brochure these days costs a great deal of money to produce, often ten or more pence a copy. The fee discourages 'literature collectors', often schoolboys, and makes a small but helpful contribution to the small operator's publicity and postage costs which otherwise would have to be recovered out of hiring fees.

If you are a beginner and have never cruised before (and don't know anyone who has who can give you personal recommendations) you are going to have to judge the firms from the brochures you receive in response to these letters. If you send all the letters out in the same post, you can make your first judgment on the length of time the firms take to reply. An efficient firm will reply promptly to your inquiry. It is best simply to ask for the firm's brochure without asking, in your first letter, any detailed questions. Usually, you will find that the brochure answers *all* the general questions, and you can subsequently write for any special information you require. Once again, you can judge the efficiency of the firm by the promptness and thoroughness with which your questions are answered. You must, however, remember that the main bulk of hire cruiser bookings are made between January and March and during these months small firms particularly are often deluged with inquiries and correspondence, and a little delay in replying to your own inquiry may be forgiven.

The brochures you receive in reply to your inquiries will conform, broadly, to a pattern. They will contain general information on waterway holidays, specific information on the waterways served by the firm concerned, and full details, usually accompanied by photographs and plans, of the craft offered for hire and the cost of hiring. Many firms include in the brochure a chart showing which boats are booked, and which are available, at the time of your inquiry. Brochures will vary from elaborate publications in full colour to quite simple black-and-white leaflets. They will enable you to take a further

9 *Above*) Luxurious interior of a modern Nauticus narrow beam canal cruiser. Twin dinette units convert to single berths at night; two further singles forward can be curtained off. Cooker in foreground; (*below*) hire cruiser leaving a narrow lock at Napton on the Oxford Canal. Note crew member left behind to close top gate after boat has left the lock.

10 (*Above*) Waterways Museum at Stoke Bruerne in Northamptonshire (last building on right) attracts 40,000 visitors a year. Dummy lock at left houses historic narrow boat in weighing machine once used to ascertain weight of cargo for toll calculations; (*below*) shortened narrow boat, converted into a roomy hire cruiser, passing the *Globe Inn* near Leighton Buzzard in Bedfordshire. Bluff bows show that this hull once worked the river Severn.

step in deciding which firm is to have your patronage, for you can be reasonably sure that the efficiently laid out and informative brochure which provides you with all the information you need for holiday planning indicates an efficient well-organised firm, and the scruffy, poorly presented brochure which doesn't give you the full story indicates one that is badly organised and less efficient.

Obviously, the larger firms will be in a position to produce more elegant and colourful brochures than their smaller competitors. This does not mean that they are necessarily more efficient, and certainly you can reasonably expect more personal attention and individual care from smaller firms, often family concerns, than from the giants. Be cautious of 'part-time' operators with only one or two boats and no proper premises, running hire craft as a sideline without the facilities to give you prompt service if you are in mechanical or other trouble during your cruise. Their hire charges may be attractively low at first sight, but this can be a poor saving.

With the brochures in front of you, you can set about choosing a boat. The size you need will be determined by the number of people in your party. The most popular hire craft are 2-, 4- or 6-berth boats, but there are also available larger craft sleeping 8, 10 or even 12 people. Often, an extra person can be accommodated aboard for a small extra charge (this usually involves sleeping the extra person in a make-shift bunk somewhere, or even simply on a mattress on the floor) but it does mean that the couple with one youngster can squeeze cheaply into a 2-berth boat, or the family of 5 squeeze into a 4-berth, without having to hire a more expensive boat than they really need simply to gain an extra berth. Most firms quote the cost of the boat per week, though some quote per person. Larger boats are cheaper per head than smaller, and two couples joining forces will spend appreciably less on hire charges (and fuel) than if they hired two 2-berth craft. In an endeavour to encourage trade outside popular bookings months, hire firms divide the season into different periods, and offer substantially reduced terms early and late in the year.

There is another factor in the amount of boat you get for your money which should be understood by the intending holiday skipper. Broads and Thames boats are nearly all appreciably wider than canal hire cruisers. This is simply because canal craft are governed by the width of the narrowest locks through which they have to pass, and cannot exceed 7 ft in beam. By contrast, other holiday craft are rarely less than 8 ft in beam, and often go up to 10 or 12 ft. This allows for roomier layouts and for some really skilful interior designs. Canal boats, accordingly, have to achieve spaciousness by becoming longer and need, for example, 40 ft to offer similar accommodation to a Broads or Thames 30-footer.

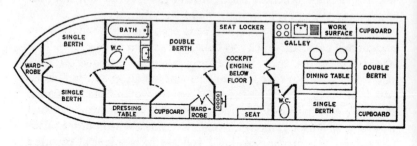

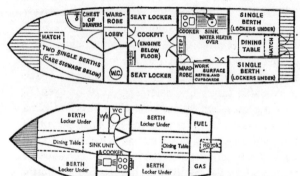

Fig 6   Three inland hire craft accommodation plans: *Top,* six/seven berth diesel-engined Broads and Thames type cruiser—40 ft long × 10 ft beam. Spacious layout includes cabin with double berth and separate bathroom and dressing-room. Galley has every mod con and whole boat is warmed by central heating system. *Centre,* typical four-berth narrow beam canal cruiser, 27 ft × 7 ft. Similar galley facilities but much tighter layout. Small petrol inboard engine. *Bottom,* small 20 ft outboard cruiser, sleeps two in cabin with optional two extra under canopy in cockpit. All basic essentials are included and cheap to hire

Apart from size, there are many different types of boat available. Unquestionably the most popular is the centre wheelhouse cruiser, with wheel positioned amidships and (usually) the engine under the cockpit floor. This pattern provides a natural break in the accommodation and separates forward from aft cabins: useful when children have to be put to bed early in that crew activities (or festivities) can continue in the other cabin without waking them. Very often the lavatory (whether pump or chemical) opens out of this wheelhouse, so that it can be reached independently from either forward or aft cabins, a useful design feature. Other types are aft cockpit or forward control craft. Both of these mean what they say and the choice will be personal.

The holiday hire skipper will also have to be chief engineer as well, so he will want to know what kind of engine will be in his care during the cruise. Most hire craft, and all the larger ones, are powered by inboard engines. Smaller craft are sometimes powered by outboards. Looking after an inboard or outboard engine presents no problems and no one need be anxious on this score. Hire cruiser engines generally are reliable units (they have to be) and very little in the way of daily maintenance attention is required from the hirer. Inboard engines will be either petrol or diesel; outboards use a mixture of petrol and oil. Diesel fuel is appreciably cheaper than petrol but diesels are noisier than petrol engines and the fuel is smelly. Good installation by the boatbuilder can overcome these problems and, eventually, diesel will certainly predominate. At the moment, many hire operators prefer petrol engines, particularly in smaller craft where problems of overcoming noise and smell are more difficult.

All that the skipper-engineer normally has to do each day is check oil level on the dipstick, give a turn to a couple of greasers, make sure there's plenty of fuel in the tank, and press the starter button. In the event of engine trouble, *don't* try to fix it yourself, and don't hire a mechanic to look at it off your own bat. If you break down out in the wilds find the nearest telephone and report to the boatyard. They will either send someone out to you or advise you what action to take. If you can get to any boatyard, do so: most yards are linked in a mutual service network and they will deal with the problem for you, contacting your boatyard if they think it necessary. Pay particular attention to any instructions covering breakdown or emergency procedure in the 'navigation hints' sent to you before your cruise. If you follow these you will get the quickest possible service. Remember that if your engine breaks down as a result of your own negligence (failure to check oil levels, watch warning instruments, or failure to carry out other recommended procedures) you *may* be held liable for the ensuing damage, so be sure you do what you are told is necessary for the care of your engine. It is in your own interest, anyway, to make sure that you don't waste cruising time for avoidable reasons. In

93

general, thoughts of mechanical disasters can be banished from the holiday skipper's mind. You are no more likely to have engine trouble afloat than in your car on the road.

Outboard engines require no daily maintenance: all you have to do is pull the starter cord or press the starter button. If they break down, the boatyard will usually simply bring you a replacement engine and take the trouble back for sorting out in the workshop.

Having looked at boat plans and specifications in several brochures, you will probably not have much difficulty in picking out a cruiser you like the look of, and you will next want to know what sort of equipment you will find aboard, and what you will need to take with you.

Most cruisers are offered for hire fully equipped with everything essential for the number of people for which the boat is designed. Most brochures give specimen inventories for the craft listed. Generally, the boat will be offered complete with all mattresses, blankets and pillows. Linen—sheets, pillow-cases, towels, tea-cloths and table-cloths—may be included or may be offered as an optional extra, for some people prefer to take their own. All necessary china, cutlery, cooking utensils and kitchen tools will be included. For safety, however, take your own favourite kitchen knife, a tin opener and a good corkscrew/bottle opener.

The specification will tell you what fixed equipment is available aboard: refrigerators are now common, many craft have running hot and cold water, most have full-size gas cookers with ovens, and many have showers or even baths. All of these make for more comfortable cruising, but boats with them will be more expensive to hire than the simpler craft without such luxuries. Gas fires can sometimes be hired; it's useful to have one if you are cruising in the spring or autumn, but *never* use it with all windows and doors shut, and *never* go to sleep leaving a gas-fire burning.

When packing to go away on a boating holiday it is best, particularly if you are going in a smallish boat, to use canvas grips rather than bulky rigid suitcases, as these stow away in less space when empty. (This is why seamen use kitbags.) However, most boatyards will store empty suitcases ashore while you are afloat, or, if you are leaving your car at the yard, you can always unpack aboard and leave the empty cases in the car.

You will want mainly informal clothing, but it is pleasant to have at least one clean and tidy outfit for dining out or other civilised activity. You will want a sweater for warmth on chilly evenings and a good waterproof just in case it should ever rain during an English summer. You will certainly want non-slip shoes and all boat shops and many shoe shops stock these. Tennis shoes or the like will serve quite well in dry weather, but can slip on wet decks. Gum boots are worth taking for muddy towpaths or crossing fields of long wet grass, but it is safer not to wear them on board—things are weighted against you if you fall in. Bird watchers (both kinds) will find field-glasses useful and camera enthusiasts should take plenty of film with them. Some films are still hard to get except in towns and the canal explorer particularly should have plenty of film with him.

A small first-aid kit and a sewing kit are worth taking, and a good torch is essential.

So much for personal equipment: how about ships' stores? Most hire boatyards run a provisions service, so that all you have to do is send in your stores list a few days before your holiday begins. The boatyard will pass the order to local suppliers who will deliver everything aboard in time for your arrival. Usually the boatyard pays the shopkeeper for you, and simply adds the cost of provisions to your cruise account. But there's nothing to stop you taking it all with you if you prefer your local grocer. Don't buy too much in the first place —you really only need provisions for the first couple of days. One of the pleasures of cruising is shopping ashore and this rarely presents any difficulties.

Remember to take with you, or to add to your stores order, essential household items such as soap, washing-up liquid or powder, dish-cloth or mop, disinfectant and toilet paper. A small roll of cheese-cloth (from most garages), or some clean rags, are well worth taking and so is a large packet of paper handkerchiefs—the bigger the better.

We've now looked at the sort of things most people want to know before they decide to go on a boating holiday. As you will have seen, there's nothing very complicated and we'll assume you decide that a cruising holiday is for your family this year. What do you do next?

In the brochure of the firm you have selected as favoured candidate for your holiday money you will find a booking form. Fill this in carefully, preferably in bold block letters. You will probably find that the form asks you to list alternative choices of both boat and holiday dates. Give as many choices as possible: the boatyard will always take the choices in order of preference. Failure to give second choices can delay confirming arrangements and perhaps lose you the chance of what would have been an acceptable alternative. Remember, people book early and the later you leave it the less choice will be open.

You will be required to sign the booking form and your signature binds you to acceptance of the Conditions of Booking of the firm concerned. You should therefore read these carefully, in your own interest, and be sure you understand the contract you are signing. Conditions do not vary much from firm to firm, and most are sponsored and approved by one or another trade association. The conditions are usually not onerous, but they are designed to protect the owner, not the hirer.

The two most serious liabilities you assume when you accept these conditions are (a) liability to pay the full hire fee, even if you are prevented from taking the holiday and have to cancel it; and (b) full responsibility for the value of the vessel and its equipment whilst on hire to you. Before you blench with horror, however, be reassured that you are offered protection against the full implication of both these serious liabilities.

Firstly, liability to pay the full hire fee. Hire operators insist on this clause to protect them against irresponsible people who might otherwise book a boat in a fit of enthusiasm and then, later, perhaps quite near the date of the booking, change their minds and go off to Bognor or Biarritz instead, leaving the boatyard with an empty boat and no chance to re-let it. They can still do this, but the boatyard can claim the hire fee and thereby avoid loss of income. Which is perfectly fair. For those who have to cancel a booking for other, and genuine reasons, all reputable holiday firms offer some form of cancellation insurance, sometimes at an additional charge, sometimes included in the cost of hire. Under this insurance, if cancellation has to be made as a result of illness, accident, death etc in the holiday party, the contract is waived and the liability of the hirer cancelled. Terms vary from firm to firm and should be very carefully studied by the intending hirer. This insurance is vital and only a fool would ignore its benefits.

Secondly, responsibility for the value of the boat is usually limited to the first £5 or £10 of any damage resulting from an accident, the balance being covered by insurance automatically, without the hirer having to ask for this cover. Some firms do not even ask for the first £5 or £10, but most do, and require this amount to be deposited before the boat is taken out, refunding it when the boat is returned in good order. Care is needed all the same, as this insurance can be voided if the hirer is negligent and damage arises from this negligence. Negligence here would be interpreted as an action of the hirer in flagrant disregard of clear instructions given to him, either verbally or in writing, by the boatyard or waterway authority. Doing something very silly as a result of inexperience would never be counted as negligence, since boatyards specifically invite beginners and can have no complaint if beginners occasionally do the wrong thing in a moment of confusion.

For the rest, the Conditions of Hire usually merely stipulate points of detail—time and place of starting and finishing cruise, hirer's responsibility to keep equipment clean, and so on—none of which are of the same legal significance as the main points discussed above.

One other legal aspect of booking should be mentioned. When the hirer is under majority age, now lowered from 21 to 18, the boatyard will require the booking form to be endorsed by a parent or guardian consenting to the booking and accepting full responsibility on behalf of the minor for the terms of the contract. This is simply because, in law, a contract cannot be enforced against a minor and not because boatyards think that people under 18 cannot handle boats.

So, read carefully through the Conditions of Hire and make sure you understand them. If in doubt, ask the boatyard to clarify any point that bothers you. Having understood, make sure you carry out any obligations placed on you by the contract, and don't do anything the Conditions specifically forbid, like trying to cross the North Sea in a Broads cruiser.

The booking form may ask you for some additional information, such as brief details of any previous boating experience or for the name of the paper in which you saw their advertisement. It may also provide for you to order optional extra equipment which may be offered (eg portable radios, cabin heaters, linen) or books, maps and charts covering your cruising area.

When finally completed, the form is sent off together with a remittance (dreadful word, but used because it covers payments by cheque, money order, postal order, or cash) to cover the booking deposit and any extras required. This deposit, of course, is a payment on account against the total hire charge. Within a few days you should receive an acknowledgment confirming that the boat is reserved for you. This will usually be in the form of a hire invoice, setting out full details of your holiday account, and showing how much will be due for payment when you take over the boat at the beginning of your cruise. This balance is always payable at the boatyard immediately before you embark.

With this acknowledgment you may receive the booklet of cruising hints most firms send to their customers, or this may follow nearer the date of your cruise. Some firms prefer to send it a week or so before you embark on the argument that if you read it too early you will have forgotten the important parts by the time your holiday comes around. If you are cruising on canals, you should also receive a Stoppages List before your cruise, listing any lock or waterway closures for repairs during the dates of your voyage. It is very important that you do receive a copy of this and the fact that you do not should never be taken to mean that there are no stoppages. Chase it up with the boatyard: most canal firms say it is your responsibility to find out about stoppages, and disclaim any liability arising from confusion if your plans are upset by a stoppage you did not know about. Of course the boatyard will try to make sure that you know about any there may be, but it is worth while double-checking.

In due course comes the big day, and you set off for the boatyard, having remembered to turn off the gas and electricity, stop the milk and papers, lock the house securely, tell both neighbours and your local police that you are away and all the other sensible things you should do and probably, like your authors, forget to do in the final panic.

Your correspondence with the boatyard will have told you at what time your boat should be ready, and you will probably have been asked not to turn up before this time to avoid confusion. You are a helpful person, so you turn up on time and find the boat is not quite but very nearly ready, and everybody tearing about in what looks like hopeless chaos but is, in fact, highly organised chaos. Most boatyards do all their turnrounds on Saturday and most have a well-tried system to ensure that the engine is thoroughly checked, fuel, water and gas tanks replenished, all equipment cleaned and checked and the boat itself cleaned throughout and made immaculate for your occupation. All this is done to a careful timetable, but the unexpected can sometimes disrupt this schedule, and the hirer who turns up early only gets in everyone's way.

Reception routines vary from boatyard to boatyard, but most commonly the new hirer reports on arrival to the office with his bookings account. This is paid and receipted, and the office will then direct him to his boat, where luggage can be stowed away before his car is driven off to garage or car park. The hirer should then check to make sure that everything he has ordered in the way of extra equipment or provisions is indeed aboard, and that the boat's inventory of equipment is complete. This is important, particularly where you are required to sign for the boat and all equipment, since you will have to pay for missing or broken items when you return, usually out of the damage deposit, and you must therefore be sure that you are not paying for something that wasn't aboard in the first place. Usually, a complete list of equipment is displayed on board, and it only takes a few minutes to check through. Make a note of any items you cannot find, and check on these with the boatyard representative when he comes along to make sure that everything is to your satisfaction. He will either show you where they are stowed, or supply them if they are indeed missing. Check also to make sure that crockery, cutlery and galley equipment is clean. Many firms change this entirely between hirers to ensure that everything is spotless, but the most efficient yard is only as good as the worst cleaner employed. Do not hesitate to complain if anything is not to your satisfaction: give the boatyard a chance to put it right, and to apologise, then and there. If something is wrong and you don't complain you have yourself largely to blame. If a fair complaint does not produce immediate action you have every right to grumble, but *never* keep your grumbles to yourself.

When your gear is stowed and the boat checked, and everything is in order, the boatyard will send a man along to explain to you how to look after your engine, how to change a gas cylinder if you need to during the cruise, and how to use any special equipment aboard. Ask as many questions as you like: he is there to help you and he will assume you understand what he says if you don't tell him that you don't. Never be afraid to appear foolish by asking what you think an elementary question. Boatyards offering hire craft are used to novices, earn their living from them, and do not expect them to be First Sea Lords. It is in the boatyard's interest, just as much as your own, that you should understand everything clearly, so ask and keep on asking.

When you are satisfied that you know all about the boat, you will be taken for a demonstration cruise. This is to show you that the boat and its controls all work, and to give you a chance to handle it with an expert aboard to correct and advise. Most people get the hang of steering a straight course fairly quickly and the demonstration run doesn't take very long. As soon as both the skipper and the boatyard representative are happy that the skipper knows what he's doing, the pilot is dropped and you're on your own. Nasty moment, but it soon passes and confidence builds rapidly.

As Chapters 4 and 5 deal in detail with the practicalities of cruising it is necessary here only to outline briefly the most common procedures on returning to base at the end of a hire cruising holiday. The first point to stress is that the time of your return is stipulated in your hire contract, and it is your responsibility to be back then. This means *being* back, not just hoping to be, if all goes well. It is your clear responsibility to allow a contingency margin in planning your cruise to make sure that there is time in hand to be back at base punctually even if you do lose cruising time as a result of mishap. Therefore choose a mooring for your last night afloat that is quite near the boatyard, to give you plenty of time for sprucing up the boat and getting back in comfortable time. This really is very important, and you must remember that someone else's holiday depends on your being back on time. Most boatyards rightly take a serious view of late returners and are within their rights to charge extra if you are late.

The second point to remember is that it is your responsibility to return the boat and its equipment in a clean condition. Make sure that everything is washed up tidily, all bedding neatly piled, and the boat decently clean. This, for most people, is a matter of simple self-respect, but there are, alas, those who are not so scrupulous. Boatyards make it their business to note in their records the state in which you return the boat. You will be welcome next year if you return on time and with everything shipshape; you will be less welcome, and may even be refused, if you did not bother to observe these requirements.

What happens when you arrive back at the base varies from yard to yard. Most commonly, however, a boatyard representative will check you in, noting any damage to the boat or its equipment, any inventory items missing, and the amount of fuel remaining in your fuel tank. The cost of any damage and the value of missing items are debited to you; the value of remaining fuel is credited. You then proceed to the office where the damage deposit is refunded to you after the debits and credits have been brought into account. Some yards will check the boat item by item in your presence; others simply ask you to declare damage or losses and take your word for it; others again do the checking after you have departed and post a refund cheque on to you.

Handling a hire cruiser is mainly a matter of common sense and no one need feel diffident about having a go. A cruising holiday is a wonderful break from routine and one of the few adventurous things that can be done by all the family. If you haven't tried inland cruising for your holiday yet you have been missing some wonderful experiences. If you are thinking about it now—a final reminder: hurry up, most firms book early.

CHAPTER SEVEN

Buying a Boat

For the beginner, buying a boat can be rather a worrying experience. There are so many different types available, new and second-hand, from boatyards, from marine traders, from private sellers via classified advertisements, that it is difficult for him to make up his mind in the confident knowledge that he will be making the 'best buy'. What would be right for one family in one area would be quite wrong for another elsewhere: the choice in the end must be personal and may well be simply solved by falling in love with a particular craft. The following may help you to consider the factors involved and tells you something about the 'where' and 'how' of setting about bringing a boat into the family.

Although the financial aspect of buying a boat is one of the biggest factors governing choice, it is not the first to be thought about. First and foremost, what do you want a boat *for*? What use do you expect to be able to get *from* it? Factors here are how many people in the family, how much they are likely to want to go boating, and how much leisure time is available for cruising. A boat big enough to sleep all the family in reasonable comfort will enable you to go for a long cruise during the family summer holiday (and the saving on hotel or other holiday expenses can be quite a material factor in the annual budget of private boating), but if you work a six-day week and only have a few spare Sundays for boating during the rest of the year you might be wiser to go for something smaller and less costly and use it only as a day boat.

Again, the type of water available locally must be very carefully considered. If you live in the Midlands you are likely to get more use out of a boat specially designed for (or at least of suitable dimensions for) canal cruising, that you can keep fairly near to home, than out of a bigger boat which has to be kept on distant, wider waters. If there are only two or three in the family, and you like and can afford distant explorations, a small cruiser that can easily be trailed behind

102

your car puts all the waters of Britain (and even Europe) within your reach.

Inevitably, your choice must to some extent be a compromise and it is likely that after a year or so you will outgrow your first boat and will want to change it for another in any case. The second is much easier to choose, and by then you will be experienced and will have discovered exactly what you want from your boat, and what you want to do with it. Most people change their boats several times, so that it is by no means a disaster if experience shows that the first choice was not the right one.

If you are a beginner it is difficult even to visualise the kind of boating that would best suit you without some fairly detailed knowledge of the kind of boat available, where you can use it, where you can keep it, how big it will be, what it will cost to buy and what it will cost to run and to maintain. So once you have decided in general terms that you would like to be a boat owner, the best thing is to do a little market research for yourself. Subscribe to the boating magazines. Visit as many boatyards, boat dealers, and general boating centres as possible and have a look at what is available.

Most boatyards offering craft for sale are open at week-ends and quite late on week-day evenings in summer and you will usually find yourself welcome to walk round without being pestered by over-keen salesmen. Often such yards will offer private moorings and a few words with a private owner aboard his own boat will tell you whether the yard is efficient and reliable and whether you could buy there with reasonable confidence.

You will usually find that a boatyard or boat dealer will have a selection of both new and used craft. The new boats may be built by the yard itself, to its own distinctive design or may be 'factory built' craft for which the yard is a selling agent, just as your local garage is an agent for factory built cars of different brands. The used craft offered for sale will sometimes be boats that the yard has taken in part-exchange and sometimes 'brokerage' sales, ie privately owned boats put into the hands of the boatyard for sale just as houses are sold by estate agents. It is important to understand this difference between used craft offered, as although the yard may well be prepared to give some form of guarantee with used craft which they sell direct, they are less likely (for obvious reasons) to give such a guarantee in the case of brokerage craft.

This means that it is up to you as buyer to satisfy yourself as to the condition of the boat you are buying, and if you are a complete beginner you will probably need some knowledgeable help here. You can obtain this professionally from a marine surveyor or, less expensively but perhaps less reliably, from an experienced boating friend. The yard should be able to give you the names and addresses of qualified surveyors or you can obtain these yourself again from the pages of the boating magazines. For obvious reasons, the person surveying should not in any way be connected with the seller. The cost of the survey will depend on the size and type of boat, whether machinery is to be included, and the distance the surveyor has to travel. If you are considering buying an oldish boat of traditional build it is always wise to have a professional survey though with a newish modern cruiser the advice of an experienced and really practical boat owner may suffice. In any case, the seller should be able to give you a fair picture as to condition and tell you whether the boat would be likely to pass a qualified inspection.

Even though a boatyard or dealer may exclude any warranty on a brokerage sale, he will have his reputation as a reputable businessman to uphold and you should be able to rely on him to point out such faults as he is aware of. No reputable yard should knowingly sell as sound a boat that is not so and for this reason any reputable yard will welcome an independent survey before a sale, as a protection for both parties.

In the case of a private sale—perhaps as a result of a classified advertisement—no such reliance can be placed on the seller and an independent inspection is essential here unless you have enough knowledge to carry out your own. If you are a complete novice, it is almost certainly best to buy your first boat from an established boat business, to be sure of good advice and to have an organisation to turn to in the event of troubles or difficulties in your early days. A further reason for dealing with a business rather than a private individual is that you will be able to obtain financial assistance much more readily in purchasing from an established trader than in making a private buy.

Finance for boat purchase is available as readily as for car or house purchase and very often such financial assistance can make possible the purchase of a more expensive boat than immediate funds would cover, and thus enables you to make a better buy. For in boats as in most other things, the cheapest initially is not always necessarily the cheapest in the long run.

Buying a Boat

Money to help with the purchase of a boat can be raised through a variety of sources. The simplest is a *bank loan*, of which there are two types. The first is simply an arrangement between you and your bank manager for an agreed sum by way of overdraft against which the manager might (or might not) want some form of security: perhaps share certificates, property deeds or the like. This is the cheapest loan you can get and interest is calculated only on the amount actually borrowed on the day-to-day balance. In general, this is for the prosperous existing customer who does substantial business with the bank rather than for the humbler customer with the more modest account. On such a loan the manager will not want to know the details of the proposed purchase: he will simply be extending a facility to a known customer. However, since the introduction of credit restrictions by the Government, overdraft facilities for personal borrowing have been severely curtailed and interest charges—if such a facility were granted—would be likely to be 3 per cent above normal bank rate, or 10 per cent at the time of printing.

To meet the needs of the more modest customer (and to pick up some of the business they were otherwise losing to hire-purchase companies) the banks a few years ago introduced the Personal Loan scheme. Unfortunately, Government credit restrictions have subsequently forced the banks virtually to close down this facility for the time being, though no doubt they will restore it as a service to customers when the economic climate improves and the Chancellor again 'takes the brakes off' consumer spending. The Personal Loan differed from a straightforward overdraft (or bank loan as described above) in that a special loan account would be opened for you by your bank, which would require you to sign an authority to the bank to make regular agreed transfers from your normal bank account over a fixed period to clear the loan. If banks were able to offer this service generally again, interest would probably be at 8 per cent and this can no longer be set off against income tax. Moreover, at present, the same regulations as apply to Hire Purchase transactions would apply to a Personal Loan if it were available: the bank could not lend in excess of two-thirds of the value of the goods and the loan would have to be paid off in a maximum of two years.

The biggest providers of funds for boat purchase are the *hire-purchase* companies, who will finance the purchase of a boat as readily as they will the purchase of a car. HP finance is only available

105

in the case of a purchase from a bona fide trader—finance companies will not assist in private transactions.

The finance company will want to know that you are a person of integrity to whom they can lend money with reasonable confidence, and—in your own interest as much as theirs—they will want to be satisfied that you can afford to repay the loan. They will want details of your age, number of dependants, home purchase commitments, nature of job and how long you have held it and a reference from your bankers. This information is provided by you on a confidential form which is submitted with your application for a loan. As with the banks, the finance companies will not normally lend more than two-thirds of the purchase price, and sometimes less. The minimum deposit to be paid by the purchaser is fixed by Government regulations as is the period of the loan. Generally, finance companies will lend for up to two years on new boats, and up to two years or less on used craft.

In hire-purchase agreements the interest is charged on the whole amount for the whole period and will normally be about 15 per cent. Interest charges on HP debts are *not* allowable against income tax.

Finally, boat finance is available in the form of a *marine mortgage*. This is usually used where the boat concerned is fairly costly—£1,500 upwards—and is a registered vessel. The formalities here are more complex and are not usually justified in the case of low or medium priced craft. Such finance would normally be arranged by the seller and the formalities can take several weeks. Mortgages are usually at a lower rate of interest than hire-purchase loans, and may be spread over longer periods. Any established boatyard will have full details on all types of finance available for boat purchase and will handle all the necessary documents for you.

From the foregoing it will be seen that finance to assist in boat purchase is available and that it is by no means necessary to have the whole of the purchase price available in hard cash. Although the minimum necessary deposit is one-third, you can of course put down more than this and borrow less. It is simply a matter of balancing funds available against the effect on your monthly budget of loan repayments, and paying initially sufficient to reduce the loan to a level where the repayments can comfortably be afforded out of regular income.

In making this calculation it is well to remember that there will be other regular expenses to be met out of income and that some of

11 (*Above*) Hotel boats *Mallard* and *Dabchick* are luxurious conversions of former cargo craft. The pair carry 12 passengers in single and double cabins; (*below*) a corner of the saloon, with a number of things necessary to comfort. Note passageway to cabins.

12 (*Above*) Cruiser for the serious enthusiast: 45ft steel 'Cutlass' hull with glassfibre super-structure with sliding wheelhouse top. Boat has wheel and tiller steering and air-cooled diesel engine; (*below*) this 4-berth marine ply Dolphin 20 ft cruiser is suitable for inland or coastal waters.

these will fall due for payment immediately you have bought a boat, so that funds must be set aside for these. There are three such 'overheads'—insurance, waterway licence and moorings. Insurance is compulsory if the boat is subject to HP or other loan arrangements, and in any case no prudent owner would neglect it. It is difficult to give an indication of likely insurance costs, since many factors affect the annual premium. On a newish 20 ft boat in sound condition costing £1,000, cruising on inland non-tidal waters for seven months of the year, and laid up ashore for the other five, the annual premium is likely to be in the region of £20. Factors involved are the total sum insured, size of boat, water to be cruised, length of time in service, experience of owner and so on. Cover is normally comprehensive and includes £25,000 third party protection. As with finance, so with insurance: the boatyard will be an agent for one or more good marine insurance companies and will quickly obtain quotations and arrange cover for you. Or, of course, you can do this yourself through your own existing insurance contacts.

Your waterway licence will depend on the waterway on which your boat is to be kept. On the extensive canal and river system controlled by the British Waterways Board a licence for a boat up to 25 ft in length costs a maximum of £14 for a full year, and less for shorter periods. This covers the use of all locks on the system as often as you like without additional payment and represents good value. The Board also has reciprocal arrangements with some other authorities that may save you charges when you pass off their waterways. On the Thames you will need a separate licence.

Mooring charges vary widely, from a penny or two per foot of length per month for a mooring on a canal towpath to five pence per foot per week and more for a private berth in a big yacht harbour or marina with every convenience and service to hand. Local inquiries in the area where you propose to keep your boat will soon establish the likely cost of moorings for your own boat.

In addition to these three immediate overhead charges of boating-insurance, licence and mooring fees—there will follow, of course, the expenses of cruising and of maintenance. The cost of cruising will not be great—simply fuel, food and such shore expenses as you care to become involved in—but it is fair to disregard these on the argument that if you were not boating in your leisure time you would be likely to be involved in some other pastime incurring, probably, more rather than less expense.

So the last unknown on the financial side, when you consider buying a boat, is the future cost of maintenance. This will depend very much on the kind of boat you buy, and whether you are able to carry out the work involved yourself or prefer to have it professionally undertaken. Generally, the more modern the boat you buy, the less it will cost you in maintenance. Old-fashioned craft of traditional construction require more attention to keep them in good trim than modern craft, and cost very considerably more to restore if they are allowed to fall into bad repair through neglect.

Though individual builders, who specialise in craft to order, still build outstanding craft on traditional lines, it is true that two modern materials have come to dominate the field in factory-built craft—marine plywood and glassfibre. Both of these materials make possible the construction of light, strong hulls requiring a minimum of framing and both (if properly used) can be fashioned into craft that cannot leak, since they have no joints or seams. This is literally true in the case of glassfibre hulls, which are moulded in a single unbroken skin and, thanks to the properties of modern resin adhesives, virtually true in the case of plywood hulls. The big difference between the two materials is that whereas plywood is organic, and will rot if not protected against moisture by paint properly applied and regularly maintained, glassfibre is an inorganic material and requires no maintenance for its protection. This means that, though it may well be more expensive in the first instance, quality for quality, it will certainly be less costly to maintain in the long run. Already glassfibre dominates the small boat field and is running neck and neck with plywood in the cruiser market. There can be little doubt that eventually it will dominate this market as well.

What this means is that if you buy a glassfibre boat of good quality you may, in a season or so, decide to paint it to restore it to new appearance and to cover the evidence of occasional bumps and scrapes; if you buy a plywood (or planked timber) boat you *must* paint it at least every second year to ensure that the timber is protected. And if you neglect to paint it, the boat will very soon begin to deteriorate. However, maintaining the paint of a modern boat is not a big job and a couple of week-ends and a few pints of paint will deal with the problem quite effectively. But it is worth bearing in mind.

The other main division between types of boat suitable for inland cruising, is the choice between inboard and outboard engine. Even the most cursory glance at craft available for sale will show that outboard power dominates the market for craft up to about 25 ft and that thereafter the inboard engine takes over. There are several reasons for this, of which the first is undoubtedly that a boat to be propelled by an outboard is much simpler to construct than an inboard-powered vessel, and can therefore be offered for sale more cheaply. This is not to say that the boat is worse built: simply that the builder does not have to worry about making engine bearers, boring the stern post and fitting engine, propeller shaft and propeller, supplying and fitting throttle and gear controls, making a rudder and its control system, or fitting a fuel tank and piping the fuel supply. All of these are added subsequently by the purchaser, who can—if the boat is properly built—fit an enormous outboard motor for high-speed coastal cruising or a very small motor suitable for gentle inland pottering. As a result, most factory-built cruisers are outboard craft.

Certainly, the outboard has many advantages. It takes virtually no space in the boat. Being outboard, it drips no oil or fuel into the bilges. Having no propeller shaft through the bottom, there is no stern tube to leak into the boat. It makes a boat highly manœuvrable, particularly so in reverse. If its propeller becomes fouled with weed it can be tilted for quick access and the whole unit can be removed for service if required in a matter of minutes. It can easily be stored ashore when not needed. It requires very little attention when in use and produces a phenomenal amount of power for its size and weight.

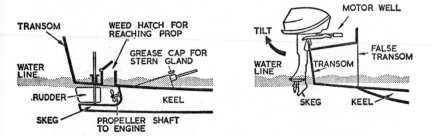

Fig 7 Typical sterngear arrangement of an inboard-engined cruiser (*above, left*) shows how the skeg extension of the keel protects propeller and rudder. Note special weed hatch (shown open here) giving access to the screw for removing weeds. Outboard cruiser (*above, right*) draws less water. Keel must be faired off to give smooth flow of water back to propeller, so gives less protection. Motor will tilt up in direction of arrow if an obstruction is hit when travelling forward (or for removing weeds) but is vulnerable to damage when going astern

But this paragon has an Achilles heel: it is very thirsty and will consume a good deal more fuel than the equivalent horse-power of inboard engine.

It is for this reason that inboards tend to take over the power at about 25 ft of boat length. At this point, in general terms, outboard power for inland craft becomes too costly in terms of fuel consumption to justify the other advantage it offers. However, 25 ft also marks another 'threshold'—the size limit at which the factory-built boat gives way to the custom-built cruiser—and beyond this limit we are moving into a class of boat which will probably be the average man's second or third cruiser.

In recent years a form of power unit offering a compromise between inboard economy and outboard flexibility has emerged in the 'inboard-outboard' transom drive. This marries a conventional inboard engine to a drive unit very much like the bottom half of an outboard motor, through the transom of the boat. For fast cruisers, this kind of unit costs about the same to install as its equivalent horse-power in outboards, and is very much cheaper to run. But as the cheapest of these units costs over £500 installed it is not yet a substitute for the low horse-power outboard for inland cruising.

So the chances are that your first boat will be an outboard cruiser, and most likely in the 18–22 ft size, and to sleep two or four people. New, this boat is likely to fall into the price range of between £500 and £1,000 'ex works and less motor'. What you will get for this money depends, of course, on the policy of the builder, but the price is likely to include mattresses for all the berths, a dining table, a cooker, a sink, a chemical toilet in the lavatory compartment, the steering-wheel and steering control system, and a canopy over the open cockpit. What will not (usually) be included are the engine, the engine controls, the gas cylinder, regulator and necessary piping to the cooker, any electric lighting, or the miscellaneous items needed to put the boat into cruising commission. A suitable outboard motor and its controls will cost anywhere between about £150 and £250 and other equipment and fittings can soon cost another £50 to achieve even minimum 'cruisability'.

Thus a new outboard cruiser priced initially at, say, £500 'ex works' will probably cost £750 by the time it is fitted out for cruising. This is not because the marine world enjoys urging you to spend extra money, but simply because when the boat is built the builder does not know if it will finish up at sea with twin 75 hp motors and three water skiers behind it, or chuffing gently down the 'cut' with Mum and the kids at a hairy 4 mph with a following wind. So the builder prices the boat with minimum essential gear and leaves the buyer to add the rest to taste.

The choice of a suitable engine and necessary extras is often confusing to a beginner, and here the advice of a good boatyard is invaluable. Boatyards are used to helping beginners through this maze and will always set out for you quotations covering essential equipment, and other items they may advise you to include for safer and more enjoyable cruising. Shop around from one yard to another, and buy from the one that is most helpful, strikes you as honest, and obviously has the equipment and know-how to back sales with proper service afterwards. Beware the yard that urges you to spend more than you can afford: a good salesman wants you to come back to him for your next boat and will take as much interest in helping you to get afloat in what is right for your needs, your family and your budget as you do yourself.

Finally, remember that if you cannot afford the right boat new, you may be well advised to look for a good used version of the same model rather than to get something smaller which you may be able to afford but which is not really big enough for your requirements. And before you sign, make quite sure your wife likes it too. . . .

CHAPTER EIGHT

Narrow Boats and their Conversion

The biggest boat that can travel over the major part of our inland water network is the traditional 'narrow boat' of the Mid-
land canals. Originally, the narrow boat was horse-drawn and
the design and dimensions of this elegant craft were such that it
exactly fitted, with only a few inches to spare, into the narrow lock
chambers of the early canals. This restriction gave the narrow boat a
maximum length of between 70 and 72 ft and a maximum beam of 7
ft. Though later canals were dug with wider locks, the narrow boat
remained the standard cargo vessel, working singly through the locks
on the narrow canals and in pairs through those on wider waterways.

Horse towing remained the major form of traction until well into
this century, when first the steam engine and later the diesel engine
took over. With self-propulsion, the design of the powered vessel
altered a little and narrow boats began regularly to work in pairs, the
powered boat towing a 'butty' which was (and remains to this day)
simply a horse boat towed not from the bank but by another boat.

Because the narrow boat is the biggest that can cruise the canal
system, and because it is the traditional canal boat, many people have
acquired former working craft and converted them into delightful
houseboats or large cruisers, often of great elegance both in internal
design and layout and in exterior appearance, retaining the colourful
and traditional decorative paintwork so beloved by the genuine canal
boatmen.

This traditional canal art, handed down from one generation to the
next and of uncertain origin, survives today as one of our few genuine
folk arts and there can be few people unfamiliar with its main 'roses
and castles' theme so often illustrated in books and magazine articles.
Small wonder that the traditional narrow boat, resplendent in its
colourful paint and adorned with polished brasswork, white rope
decoration and even horses' tails streaming from rudder posts,

114

should attract the enthusiasm of those looking for a roomy and unusual inland waterway boat.

However, attractive though it may be, the full-length narrow boat is hardly a beginner's boat. Steering a 70-footer round the bends and curves of a shallow canal is an acquired skill, and if the boat has a full-length cabin and the day is windy, even the most skilful will be hard taxed to stay in mid-channel and get safely through small bridges without damage. It should also be remembered that 70 ft is a lot of hull to keep in good condition, that dry docking will be necessary and that accordingly a substantial budget for maintenance will be necessary if the boat is to be kept in good condition.

As we saw earlier, there are two types of narrow boat: the tug, or motor-boat, and the towed boat or butty. These differ only at the stern and, indeed, the early motor boats were simply horse boats modified to accommodate an engine. The butty boat is double-ended and steered by a large wooden rudder hung on the stern post. It has a small cabin aft, an open hold about 50 ft in length, and a small foredeck. When empty it floats level in the water.

The motor-boat has a rounded counter stern, with the propeller below, and is steered by a metal rudder partially below and partially behind this counter. It also has a small living cabin aft and just forward of this a separate compartment for the engine. Because the propeller shaft must pass below the floor of the living cabin, thus raising it, the cabin of a motor is higher and narrower than a butty cabin. Forward of the engine-room again is the open hold, usually about 40 ft in length, and right forward a similar foredeck. Because of the overhanging counter and the weight of the engine and fuel, a motor boat draws more water aft and does not float level when empty but slopes 'downhill' from forward to aft. Thus it will be seen that a butty boat—with some 10 ft more of hold space available for turning into living accommodation and floating level in the water—is to be preferred for conversion into a static houseboat not required to move under its own power, and a motor-boat hull is preferable for conversion to a cruising boat. (It is perfectly possible to fit an engine into a butty boat, utilising the original living cabin as an engine-room and modifying the stern and rudder to accommodate a propeller, but obviously a more elaborate and expensive operation than starting with a proper motor-boat hull.)

Originally, all narrow boats were built of wood, oak for the side planks, stem and stern posts and knees, and elm for the bottoms.

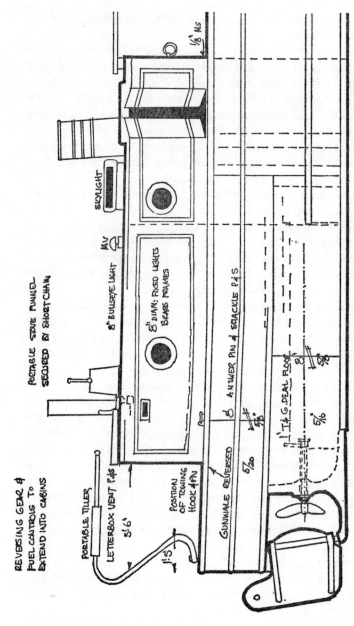

Fig 8 Detail from 1935 construction drawing of steel motor narrow boats built at Woolwich for the Grand Union Canal Carrying Co Ltd. Some of these craft are still in cargo service and in excellent condition. This is a 'composite' boat with steel sides and 3 in elm bottom, the easiest type to shorten

Apart from slight local variations of line, the design was standard and the method of construction remained unchanged for nearly 200 years. The last wooden narrow boat to be built for commercial service was launched from the then Samuel Barlow dock at Braunston in the late 1950s, and is still in regular cargo service. Wooden canal boats, properly maintained, had an astonishingly long life expectancy. Many of them worked for thirty years and some, converted to houseboats, are still afloat and in regular use fifty years after they were built. Between the wars, with the formation of the Grand Union Canal Carrying Company, a big effort was made to modernise narrow canal carrying, and many narrow boats were built of all-steel or 'composite' construction—steel-sided with wooden bottoms of 3 in thick elm. Such narrow-boat carrying as survives today is almost (but not quite) entirely operated by these steel craft which, of course, require less maintenance than wooden craft.

Probably the most difficult step in acquiring a converted narrow boat for private use these days is the first one of finding a suitable hull. Unless you are very lucky, you are now unlikely to find for sale an unconverted wooden hull in good enough basic condition to justify the fairly heavy expense of conversion. Unfortunately, long after they should have known better, canal boat docks persisted in using black iron nails and fastenings in the construction of wooden narrow boats. Oak contains tannin which, in the form of tannic acid, attacked the iron and caused rust. As the nails and bolts rusted, so they fitted less tightly in the timber and in seeped the water, accelerating the rust process and starting decay in the timber itself. The fractional additional expense of using galvanised fastenings in the first place would have saved canal operators thousands of pounds, but curiously—such was the hold of tradition—they would have no truck with new-fangled ideas. As a result, few good wooden hulls survive and even those that do will require constant maintenance and plank renewal.

Without doubt, if you contemplate an expensive conversion, wait until you can find a good all-steel or composite boat. Even if the steel is thin in places, patches can be welded on and these will be unlikely to need further attention in a lifetime. Similarly, even if the wooden bottom of a composite boat needs the renewal of some planks, these are simply bolted to the steel sides and renewal is perfectly straightforward.

Although the 70 ft length of a narrow boat offers maximum space

117

for cabin accommodation when converted, this length can be a bit of a problem. Not only are full-length boats tricky to handle, but they can only be turned at infrequent intervals where a canal junction or special wide place (known as a 'winding hole'—pronounced to rhyme with the wind that blows) offers enough water to turn a 70-footer. This means that they are not suitable for a casual cruise, where you turn and head back home when the fancy takes you. As a result, many people who like the idea of owning a proper narrow boat but wish to avoid the problems of a full-length one have chosen to shorten such a hull to more manageable proportions.

There are various ways in which this may be done, but it is an operation calling for a good deal of plant and know-how and is not really for the amateur. A popular method is to take a butty boat (which, as we have seen, is double ended) and to cut this in half, giving two 35 ft sections. To the raw ends of each section is added, either by building on or fixing on a prefabricated unit, a motor-boat type stern. The front half, of course, already has the existing bow section and forms a perfect miniature motor-boat after the operation. The stern half has its original rudder and cabin removed, and the old pointed stern end becomes the bow of the new boat. If the job is well done, the sale of the unwanted half can go far to offset the purchase and conversion costs of the whole exercise.

A more common method of achieving a shortened narrow boat, however, is to take a motor-boat and simply cut out a section amidships and then rejoin the two ends. This *can* be done with a wooden boat but is a fairly major job since it would be unsatisfactory simply to cut out a section and try to butt-joint all the planks on a single line. Planks must be removed carefully so that when the two ends are drawn together, the plank ends interlock like the fingers of two hands brought together. But the operation is most simply, most invisibly and most quickly carried out on a composite boat. Here the unwanted length of wooden bottom amidships is simply unbolted and removed, the appropriate length is cut from each steel side with a cutting torch, the two ends are drawn together and the sides neatly welded. The operation is completed by bolting a single new wooden bottom into place at the joint. A moment's thought will show that the operation is much more tricky with an all-steel boat, since this can only easily be cut and joined if two absolutely identical cross sections are chosen—not an easy task in an old boat that will certainly have been slightly dented and buckled in years of cargo carrying.

118

A word of comfort here to those who fancy the idea of a traditional narrow-boat cruiser but can't find a suitable hull or are daunted by the problems involved in shortening and converting a working boat. In recent years several new firms have emerged producing brand-new wooden and steel short narrow boats specially for pleasure cruising. As the supply of genuine working boats dries up, as very soon it must, these firms can expect to prosper.

Having once obtained your hull, full length or shorter, and put it into good condition, the next problem is the cabin conversion. It is no more possible to advise on an 'ideal' conversion plan than it would be to design an ideal house. The arrangement of the interior space must reflect personal, family needs. Nevertheless, the physical size of a narrow boat itself, and of the bridges under which it must pass, impose a certain discipline, and some general notes may be of assistance to those planning a conversion.

The height of the cabin sides should not exceed about 3 ft 6 in above the gunwales of the hull, and the cabin top should not be wider than 4 ft 6 in to 5 ft. If you are building on a motor-boat hull, the lines of the existing cabin cannot be bettered and this should simply be extended forward. Windows should be positioned so that their sills are as low as possible, to make it possible to see out easily when sitting down. They may be of the sliding type (which have to be closed when it is raining because of the slope of the cabin sides but through which you can put your head or empty the teapot) or of the hopper type, tipping inwards, which can be left open in the rain but through which you *cannot* put your head, etc. They should *never* be of the hinged type, whether side or top hung, or sooner or later they will be ripped off in a lock, quite apart from being a danger to anyone walking along the gunwales. If the windows are not big enough or not suitable to allow you to get out of them in a fire, make sure your layout plan provides for exits at both ends of the cabin. A roof hatch will suffice for one of these, as long as it is accessible and opens easily.

If possible, have an open well-deck right forward with raised floor and seats so that people can sit and see while cruising. This can have an awning for rain and night time. This is the quietest spot in the boat and quite the pleasantest place to sit while travelling. If you can arrange this, then the first cabin should be made the saloon, so that the well-deck forms an open-air extension to this for summer living, and a handy place to leave oilskins (when the canopy is up) if you come in out of the rain. The saloon, of course, must incorporate the

119

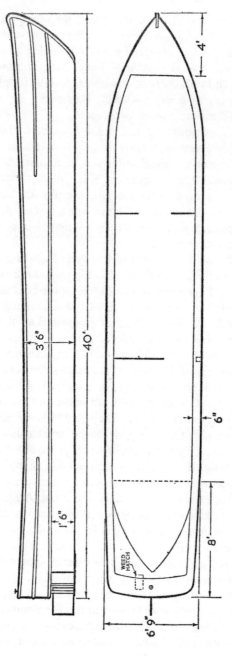

FIG 9 The growing demand for canal cruisers on traditional narrow boat lines coupled with a shortage of genuine narrow boats has opened a new market for traditionally-styled steel cruiser hulls. The popular length is 40 ft. The profile and plan above are of 'Cutlass' steel hulls

eating area, so the galley must come next, or form a part of it if you like an open plan. If you are going to use the boat early and late in the year, try to include a solid-fuel stove in the saloon. There is no substitute for a coal fire (properly enclosed for safety) for warming and drying a boat. If houseboat use is envisaged, this stove can have a back boiler for hot water and even a simple radiator system.

Beyond the galley you must incorporate lavatory and washing and/ or bathing facilities, and sleeping cabins. If you fit a flushing yacht toilet remember you cannot use this on the Thames and the time may well come when it will be forbidden on other waters. A shower is possible but complicated: it will need an electric pump to deliver the water above your head, and another to suck it away since the base tray will be below waterline. A small bath uses a little more water but if your water tanks are high up will fill by gravity and can be positioned above waterline so that it will empty without a pump.

Sleeping cabins on a cruising boat should be kept as small as possible, leaving every possible square foot free for day activities. There is room, but only just, to have cabins to one side with a passage beside them, but it is a tight squeeze.

If the boat is to be lived in during cold weather, insulate the inside of the cabin structure and hull sides with polystyrene or glass wool, panelled over, to prevent heat loss and condensation. But, particularly with a wooden hull, make sure that adequate ventilation can get behind the panelling and under floors, or rot will soon set in. *Never* lay the whole floor and build bulkheads on top of it. Build the bulkheads first and put the floor down between them, so that it can readily be lifted for access to the bottom without major dismantling of the interior. Protect all timber floor bearers, and the lower parts of bulkheads, with an anti-rot treatment, and try to keep wooden bearers clear of bilge water. One way is to lay these on blue bricks, chocked into position, putting a small square of roofing felt or builder's damp-proof course between the brick and the timber. On a steel hull, L-shaped angle irons can be welded into position to carry both floorboards and to receive the lower edge of hull panelling. The more care you take to keep the interior woodwork away from the hull and ventilated the longer the interior will last and the warmer your boat will be.

When you are fitting out, *never* run butane gas tubing behind panelling or under floors. Clip it up high, and use as few joints as possible. For preference do the same with electric wiring and *never*

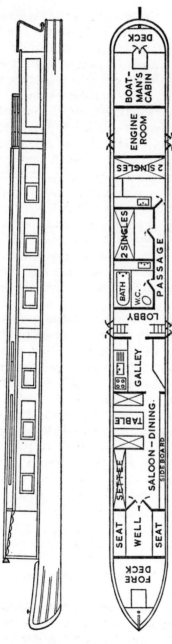

FORE DECK | SEAT | WELL | SEAT | SETTEE | TABLE | SALOON–DINING. | SIDEBOARD | GALLEY | LOBBY | BATH | W.C. | PASSAGE | 2 SINGLES | 2 SINGLES | ENGINE ROOM | BOAT-MAN'S CABIN | DECK

Fig 10 There is no such thing as an 'ideal' narrow boat conversion, but this plan (specially prepared for this book) incorporates some basic essentials. It envisages a family of six and provides space for extra guests on occasion. Well-deck forward has raised floor and wide seats which (with canopy down) could serve as extra berths. Saloon has 'dinette' arrangement seating six for meals and convertible into double berth at night. Day settee could sleep a visitor and could have 'swing up' back to make further bunk above. Galley includes large sink with h. and c., full domestic gas cooker and refrigerator. Lobby has ladders to side doors and space for coats, oilskins, etc, to hang. Bathroom includes wash-basin and toilet—flushing or chemical. Sleeping cabins both have two single berths and could include wash-basins. Hot water is from gas-fired storage heater in bathroom but could be from solid-fuel boiler sited in saloon or lobby. Water tanks are carried in central raised 'lantern' roof, which also includes small ventilator windows over saloon and galley. Large skylight over engine room serves as maintenance hatch for lifting engine ashore. Original boatman's cabin aft could be used as spare room or junk room. Note that awning over well-deck is carried on permanent framework incorporating top plank so crew can walk overhead. Tunnel headlamp is mounted in front of awning frame. Large windows slide in frames, which could in-corporate shutters for security when boat moored unattended. All windows are big enough for emergency escape. Cabin structure built either in marine grade plywood or planking capped with weatherproof hardboard

conceal junction boxes or sure enough the terminals will corrode and you will have to strip half the interior to trace a simple fault. Gas cylinders should be in a metal locker above waterline and vented outboard. If you want a gas-operated refrigerator, fit it high up so that the pilot flame is well clear of the bilges. If the boat has a petrol engine, don't use a gas refrigerator at all—or check first with your insurers that they will accept it, and take professional advice on the installation.

Clearly, it is impossible in the space of a short chapter to give a complete do-it-yourself guide to narrow-boat conversion. These notes can be no more than a warning to the complete beginner that there is more to converting a boat than might, at first, meet the eye and a quick reference to some of the more important aspects for the man with the time, the skill and the tools (not to mention the £ s d) to tackle his own conversion.

CHAPTER NINE

Maintenance

M any would-be boat owners are deterred from taking the plunge into ownership by the mistaken belief that looking after a boat requires a great deal of time and money. Obviously, the care of any capital item—whether it be boat, caravan, motor-car or even a house—requires some effort and expense, but neither need be crippling provided the boat you start with is reasonably modern and in fairly good condition. An old boat in bad condition can most certainly be a drain on the pocket but a reasonably new cruiser will not prove too demanding on leisure time or pocket.

Many owners, in fact, derive as much pleasure and satisfaction from looking after their boat and keeping it shipshape as they do from cruising, and if you are of a practical turn of mind and capable of doing the simple maintenance work a boat requires, the care of a cruiser need not cost you very much.

Maintenance comes under three headings—seasonal, winter lay-up and spring refitting, and we will look at the problems separately. First of all, it is important to stress that the principle of 'a stitch in time' applies to boats almost more than to anything else. *Never* ignore small maintenance jobs—through neglect you will find that they can become major jobs requiring major effort or professional assistance, and this can be expensive. A small deck leak, for example, should be stopped immediately, even if only temporarily with a squeeze of mastic from a tube. Failure to stop it could lead in time to waterlogged deck timbers and eventual rot.

Seasonal maintenance is mainly a matter of common sense and being tidy-minded. The first essential is to keep your boat clean, inside and out. Carry the right cleaning tools and equipment aboard— a deck mop and scrubber for outside, floorcloths, bucket, dustpan and brush for the interior. Always have a supply of clean rag aboard and if your boat has metal fittings have the appropriate polish or cleaner. When you start away from the moorings at the beginning of

13 (*Above*) 'Enclosed steering' Ormélite canal cruiser features amidships wheelhouse with sliding roof and side panels. Standard model as shown here is all-fibreglass, and larger versions are available in marine ply; (*below*) outboard-powered Inlander 25 was a 1967 newcomer to the canal scene and gained instant popularity. Fibreglass hull with plywood superstructure. The boat is built by a former caravan manufacturer.

14 (*Above*) Luxurious cabin interior of the Freeman 22. This 4-berth inboard cruiser is an inland waterway 'classic', and among the most popular and successful boats ever built. A narrow canal version, the 'Six Ten', is also available; (*below*) Norman '228 Executive' all-glassfibre 4-berth cruiser. This version is powered by marinised Ford engine by Mangoletsi and uses 'Transa-Drive' inboard-outboard propulsion system.

a cruise, and when you tie up at the end, run round the decks with a mop and plenty of water to get rid of muddy footmarks. Mud is often acid and will stain paintwork if not cleaned off. When you are mopping off, make sure that all drain holes and water run-off points are clear of dead leaves and muck and working efficiently. Stagnant pools of water trapped by blocked drain holes will soon cause trouble.

Keep your ropes and fenders in good order. The ends of ropes should be whipped or spliced, and if one of these comes undone, or a rope breaks, don't leave the ends to unwind slowly, or simply tie a knot to stop it stranding. Make a decent job of it then and there, or sling it out and get another. In any emergency, the safety of the boat can depend on good ropes, so don't ignore their care. Sisal ropes are cheap but they will rot and lose their strength in time: change them after a couple of seasons. Modern synthetic ropes are more costly to begin with, but are very strong, rot-proof and will last for ever. They have the further advantage that they require no whipping at the ends, but can be fused neatly into a terminal blob by holding the end in a gas or light flame, when all the strands will neatly melt together.

Keep metal deck fittings, window trims, horns, searchlights and the like clean and polished. Tarnished brass or chrome-work looks scruffy and unseamanlike. If exterior paint and varnish-work gets rubbed or scored, retouch it promptly to keep the weather out. Keep the hull washed down, particularly round the waterline where it can soon become discoloured and unsightly. If necessary, when the hull is oil-stained round the waterline, sprinkle a little detergent powder on the deck mop or scrubber.

Inside, keep the domestic area clean and tidy. Don't let fluff and dirt gather in corners and crevices, holding moisture and starting decay. Keep your bilges dry by pumping and mopping out regularly. Dirty bilges will begin to smell stale in time, giving the boat a seedy, musty atmosphere. Regular cleaning and drying will not take very long, but it will pay off handsomely over the years.

On the mechanical side, don't neglect your engine until it finally develops trouble. Inspect and clean it regularly: attend to oil changes and grease points as necessary and keep your battery properly topped up with distilled water. The more often you look at and work over your engine the better, for this way you are more likely to spot anything coming undone or going wrong before it advances far enough to do any damage. Traditional engine-room 'bull'—all brass fittings and copper tubes polished every day, and everything clean and shin-

ing—isn't just for show: it is tangible evidence to the Chief that someone has been all round every part of the engines every day. Once you
let the engine department get so dirty and oily that even looking at it
will cover you in mess you have a first-class incentive to ignore it, and
then your troubles start.

In this country, the summer boating season normally runs from the
beginning of April until towards the end of October, and most craft
are laid up for the winter from November to March inclusive—seven
months in commission and five laid up. When summer draws to an
end, and the time to lay-up for winter draws close, the wise owner
lays his plans with care, for winter can be a cruel time for small craft
and a neglected boat can suffer grievously through the cold, wet
months.

The first decision to take is whether the boat is to stay afloat or
come ashore for winter. There is a generally held, but quite mistaken,
belief that it is 'bad' for a boat to be out of the water for any length of
time. This goes back to the time when most craft were built of wooden
planking (either of carvel construction, with smooth planking, or
clinker built, with overlapping strakes) in which case it would happen
that the planks would dry out and shrink while the boat was ashore
and so cause leaking when she was refloated in the spring. This is
obviously a problem if the boat cannot be kept under supervision,
and pumped frequently, during the first few days afloat; thereafter
the timbers will usually soon swell and 'take up' again, when the
leaking will stop. But the modern boats with marine ply, glassfibre or
metal hulls, present no such problems and such hulls can quite safely
be hauled out and laid up on dry land with no problems on re-
launching.

Why haul out at all? There are many reasons for preferring to have
a smallish cruiser ashore rather than afloat in the winter. First of all,
once it is ashore it requires much less attention. It cannot break
adrift, as a result of storm or floods, so you can sleep easily at nights
without worrying about it. It cannot sink or be damaged by ice. It can
be sheeted right over to protect it from the weather, and it won't
grow weed and slime round the hull below water. In addition, once
it is safely ashore, all parts of the hull are accessible for maintenance
and it is much more easily worked on than when afloat.

Hauling out, however, does require the availability of suitable facilities—slipway, trailer and space for shore storage. These may not
always be available, or the boat may be too big to be hauled out and

stored ashore without prohibitive expense, so that staying afloat for the winter is unavoidable. We will examine the various recommended procedures for laying up both ashore and afloat, and if these are followed carefully, your boat will take little harm during the bad weather months.

First of all, whether the boat is coming ashore or staying afloat, it is sensible to remove anything that will be affected by the damp and cold of winter. Clothing, curtains, bedding, cushions and mattresses and any rugs or carpets are the obvious firsts. Not only will these be better in warm, dry storage at home, but getting them out of the way will make other interior maintenance aboard the boat much easier. Most of these soft furnishings will need washing or dry cleaning by the end of the season. Have this done right away instead of leaving it until the spring. Often, nowadays, cleaners send this sort of thing packed in polythene which makes for easy storage. If not, buy a few cheap polythene bags, pack the clean stuff away in the attic or spare room, and it will be all ready to go back aboard in the spring.

Paper does not like damp conditions, either, so pack the ship's library, including maps, charts and the log, into a cardboard carton and take this home too.

Cutlery, cooking tools and pots, china and glassware doesn't *have* to come ashore since it won't take any harm aboard. On the other hand, if you get rid of it you have a chance to give all the cupboards and shelves a thorough clean, and if the boat itself is going to be loaded on and off a trailer, or tipped from side to side for painting, the less loose gear aboard the better. So, for preference, load all this into cartons as well and get it home, give it a good clean, wrap it in clean newspaper and, once more, it is all ready for the spring.

If you do decide to leave domestic equipment aboard, it is worth while making sure that all cutlery and kitchen tools are washed clean, and then lightly oiling them with olive oil, wrapping them in newspaper and boxing them in a carton rather than simply leaving them in drawers and lockers. This will prevent rust and corrosion and, again, will give you easy cleaning access to their normal storage spaces.

Since the more loose gear you remove or pack into cartons the easier it becomes to work inside the boat, the real aim should be to get rid of everything possible. Having sorted the soft furnishings and domestic equipment, the marine gear comes next. Most owners find that in the course of a season the lockers where the loose gear is kept tend to become glory-holes full of odd lengths of rope, discarded fenders, odd tools, oil-cans, mooring stakes, hammers and a good deal else besides. Have it all out: chuck away the useless stuff, put on one side for attention anything that needs cleaning or mending and—for preference—take it all home and store it in a couple of boxes in the garage. Failing that, clean out the lockers it lives in thoroughly, and pack it back neatly.

The biggest enemy your boat has to face in winter is frost. Once the temperature drops below freezing-point gentle water turns to vicious ice, and—as every schoolboy knows—expands slightly but irresistibly in doing so. So the next stage is to get rid of all water aboard. In general this means dealing in turn with four aspects: first, the domestic water system, tanks, piping, water heaters, pumps, taps and sink outlets; second, the lavatory and its plumbing; third, the engine cooling system; and, finally, the bilges. All must be bone dry and must remain so throughout the bad weather.

We'll take them in order. The quickest way to empty your tanks is to break a pipe joint in the lowest part of the system and simply let them drain into the bilges. If this isn't possible, pump them to waste through the galley sink and wash-basins. If the tanks have inspection covers, take this opportunity to flush and clean them. If there are electric or hand pumps in the system, make sure these are quite dry. If possible, disconnect inlet and outlet pipes to be sure of this, and leave them off for the winter. Drain water heaters or hot water tanks in the same way. If your galley sink or wash-basins have 'traps' (ie small sump bends which contain a small amount of water to stop bad smells blowing back up the waste pipe), remove the drain plugs and empty these. Put the drain plugs and other removed fittings into the sink so that you'll remember they are out when spring comes again, and also so that you'll find them.

Yacht-type pump toilets need special care. First thoroughly flush and clean them. Next turn off the inlet seacock and pump until everything appears dry. Then turn off the outlet seacock, remove both inlet and outlet pipes and pump again. *Be certain* no water remains in bends or pump barrels. Plug the pan with a wadge of clean newspaper. Chemical toilets should be emptied and thoroughly cleaned with hot water, detergent and disinfectant until they are perfectly clean and sweet.

The engine comes next. Draining the cooling system is only one part of laying an engine up for winter, so we will deal with the whole engine lay-up routine at this point. Get hold of the manufacturer's handbook and carefully follow the instructions for laying up. If you can't get hold of one, and are in any doubt at all, get advice from a boatyard or experienced fellow-owner. The engine is the vital heart of your boat, the most expensive item aboard, and it deserves special care. The ideal, of course, is to have the engine ashore for the winter in a dry, warm workshop or garage, but this—though very simple if it is an outboard—is not so easy with the bigger inboard motors and mostly these have to stay aboard.

If the engine is in good order and running well, all you need to do is to protect it from the cold and damp, not only externally, but internally as well. If it needs an overhaul—and boat engines need regular maintenance just like car engines—the autumn is a good time to have this put in hand. Boatyards are not so busy then as in the spring and, after the overhaul, you can put the engine to bed for the winter knowing that everything is right and ready for the off in the spring.

Assuming the engine is healthy, the basic essentials are to get it clean inside and out, and keep it dry inside and out. Start with an oil change (including gear box) and a new oil filter. This will get rid of sour, acid combustion products which could cause damage if left in the engine all the winter. Next, get rid of the cooling water. Turn off the inlet seacock, take the top off the inlet filter or disconnect the cooling pipe from the seacock. Go round the engine carefully removing all drain plugs from the cooling jacket, exhaust manifold and silencer. (Put the plugs somewhere safe, where they will be easily found in the spring: in the sink with the other bits, or in a bag tied on to the engine.) If you have been cruising in muddy canals, you may find that the cooling passages are obstructed in some places with mud. Poke a piece of wire into the drain holes and see if this unblocks mud and allows water to gush out. If there does seem to be an excess of mud, or the waterways appear blocked or restricted, seek advice. It may be that the engine needs descaling, and this should not be neglected, or overheating and eventual damage will result. Disconnect the cooling pipes all round the engine to be safe, making sure no water remains in the cooling pump or in pipe bends. Then run the engine for a timed minute to dry it finally. Next, drain the silencer and make sure no water remains trapped in any bends in the exhaust. Finally, on the exhaust system—and this is most important if the boat is staying afloat—make a wooden bung to fit into the exhaust outlet and drive this firmly home. (Not *too* firmly or, after it has swollen with damp, you'll never get it out again in the spring.)

Next, take out the spark plugs or injectors, put about an eggcupful of clean engine oil (or special inhibiting oil for preference) into each cylinder and turn the engine over by hand a few times. Plug the holes with clean rag and have plugs or injectors cleaned and tested ready for next season.

Next, turn off the fuel, drain the carburettor, clean out any fuel filters and take the opportunity to give the engine a thorough external clean including the drip tray below it. (But on a diesel do *not* turn off or drain fuel system. It is better left full of oil.)

The engine's electrical system is most likely to suffer from long exposure to damp and cold. Many owners like to remove the dynamo, starter motor, ignition system (magneto, or coil and distributor) bodily for shore storage at home, but if this is not possible it is certainly worth spraying all these components and the various ignition and other electrical leads with one of the handy aerosol silicone anti-damp sprays available from marine chandlery stores or motor accessory shops. The battery should certainly be removed and stored ashore *and kept charged* through the winter.

Finally, cover the engine with a clean cloth and some old sacks or blankets and it will sleep happily all winter long and awake refreshed for another season of work in the spring.

The last item on the engine side is the fuel tank. For safety's sake the tank should be emptied for the winter and this is particularly important if the engine is a two-stroke burning an oil/petrol mix. The oil will tend to form a gummy deposit if left in the tank all winter and this can cause a good deal of jet blocking in the spring. (But empty tanks will tend to collect moisture through condensation inside so it is as well to flush them in the spring with a little methylated spirit and then with clean fuel or paraffin to wash any water out before filling up for the new season.)

If your boat has an outboard motor, it will generally pay you hands down to take this immediately the season is over to one of the maker's approved service agents for an inexpensive end-of-season service check which includes inhibiting the motor with special oil for winter storage. Modern outboards are complicated pieces of machinery packing a lot of power in a small space and the small expense of an annual service check is a sensible investment to ensure years of trouble-free cruising. The important thing is to have the motor serviced *before* the winter, and not to leave it stewing in its own juice (literally) until the spring.

But if you are a do-it-yourself man, have the necessary tools and the maker's handbook, and the motor is running well and not in need of special attention, purely routine service presents no problem Before you remove the motor from the boat, disconnect the fuel line and run the motor until the carburettor is empty and the motor stops. Lift the motor ashore, hold it upright to allow cooling water to drain and pull the starter a few times to clear cooling water from the pump. Clean off any marine growth from the lower unit. Then take the motor, tank and fuel hose home for the rest of the work and winter storage. Ideally, make a stand for the motor so that it can be stored upright in its normal position, thus allowing any moisture to drain away from the powerhead.

When you have the motor at home, put a pan under it and drain off the gearcase oil from the lower unit. If there seems to be a lot of water in this oil, you may have a failed seal on the shaft and should take the motor to an expert. If not, simply refill with fresh oil which *must* be of the type advised by the makers. Lay the engine down so that plugs are uppermost, take out the plugs and put a teaspoonful of ordinary engine oil into each cylinder. Turn the engine over a few times by hand—most easily done by putting it in gear and turning the propeller since you won't be able to reach the normal starter lanyard with the engine lying on the floor—to coat the cylinder walls with oil. Leave the pistons half-way down the bores, thus blocking off the inlet and exhaust ports, and replace the spark plugs or, in their place, fit special moisture absorbers available from any good outboard service agent for a few shillings. Stand the motor upright on its special stand, and go round all grease points with a grease gun. Empty and clean the fuel filter. Clean the motor down thoroughly, wipe it over with a clean oily rag and leave it upright until the spring. If you really want to keep the motor 'as new', buy an aerosol can of matching touch-up paint and spray over any discoloured or corroded areas before wiping over with oil. Empty the fuel hose and tank (you can use the fuel in your car as a little oil won't do any harm) and flush the tank with a little plain petrol or paraffin.

Finally, on the anti-frost campaign, the bilges. These should be pumped out thoroughly and it is sensible to make an occasion of it and give them a good clean at the same time. In a modern cruiser this is not generally a very big job, but in an older boat of traditional build, particularly if it has an inboard engine, the bilges can become quite dirty over a season and getting the dirt out from the nooks and crannies can be quite a job. Liquid detergents are a big help if the bilges are oily. It is worth while making a real job of this as damp dirty bilges are a fine starting point for rot.

If the boat has an inboard engine and is staying afloat for the winter, put plenty of grease into the stern tube and tighten the gland to prevent it dripping. When you have cleaned the bilges thoroughly, and pumped and mopped out the last of the water, make sure finally that the bilge pump itself is dry and not left with the pump chamber full of water.

Whether the boat is afloat or ashore during the winter, the bilges should be checked from time to time to make sure they remain dry. Oddly enough, a boat ashore will suffer more damage if water in the bilges freezes than a boat afloat. This is because there will be no counter-pressure from ice forming outside the boat to resist the outward pressure of ice forming inside, and the bilge ice will quietly expand and tend to push the transom out to make way for expansion.

If the boat is hauled out for winter, the first job is to scrub off all weed and growth below the waterline as the boat comes up the slipway. It will come off quite easily when wet, but will set like concrete if left to dry on the hull.

If you are sensible, and really care for your boat, you will finish off the laying up by giving the whole boat a good clean throughout, washing down paintwork inside and out, cleaning the cooker and refrigerator, and will go round all internal and external metalwork with a coat of protective oil or grease. Light fittings tend to suffer from damp corrosion and it is worth while removing bulbs, lightly greasing the brass parts and replacing them. A drop of thin oil into the moving parts of light switches also helps. This sort of thing is fiddly, but it will pay off handsomely in the long run.

When all is finished inside, leave internal doors ajar (including oven and refrigerator doors), take up floorboards, open drawers and cupboards, so that everywhere is thoroughly ventilated. If you can afford it, buy a canvas or heavy PVC storage cover to protect the upperworks from rain, snow and ice. This should be rigged over a fore and aft pole if possible, tent fashion, to allow air to circulate below it and it must be thoroughly lashed down against winter gales. Given such a sheet, cabin windows and doors can also be left ajar without fear of rain or snow entering the boat. The more breeze that can blow through, the better to keep down condensation.

A good day or a week-end towards the end of October will comfortably take care of these lay-up jobs and there is no doubt that it represents time well spent. Apart from, say, a monthly inspection to make sure all is well, you can then forget her with a quiet mind until spring sunshine tells you the time for cruising is coming round again.

Spring refitting is largely a matter of reversing all the lay-up procedure to get everything back into commission, plus any fresh painting or varnishing needed. A fresh coat of antifouling, to stop weed growth below waterline, is essential and as there are various different types of this special paint it is important to follow the paint-maker's instructions to the letter. Good weather is essential if painting and varnishing are to be carried out in the open, and timber must be thoroughly dry if the new paint is to stay on. Generally, the most important thing in painting and varnishing is thorough preparation. Loose and peeling paint should be stripped right back to bare wood, using paint stripper or blowlamp, and a proper paint build-up, undercoating and enamel, applied in accordance with the maker's instructions. Thorough sanding down between coats, to give a good 'key' for the next coat, is vital, and it is always better to apply two thin coats rather than one thick one. A good paint job not only makes the boat look better, it protects it, lengthens its life and maintains its value. One of the boat owner's deepest satisfactions is standing back from his freshly painted boat and admiring her in her new sparkling glitter. And if you are not a handyman, or haven't the time to paint your boat yourself, get a boatyard to do it for you. The expense is a good investment and you can still stand back and admire it!

CHAPTER TEN

To Help You Enjoy Your Boat

Whether you own your own boat, or are an occasional hirer, you and your family will have much more fun if you mix with others who also enjoy the water.

BOAT CLUBS

There are very many of these. Membership is mainly for boat owners, but most clubs have many non-owning members. During the summer months a typical club will organise one or two week-end rallies. A gathering point is announced, members collect, competitions are held both for the boats and for wives, children and those who turn up on the bank, with a general get-together in the evening.

Another summer activity is the cruise, perhaps over a bank holiday week-end, when members meet and cruise together on an agreed course, with bankside events laid on during the evening. Throughout the season competitions are going on for trophies (eg attendance at rallies, participation in competitions, longest cruising distance covered in the year, boat handling ability, etc) and proficiency certificates for juniors.

In the winter such clubs usually run dances, slide and film shows, dinners (pirate suppers are popular), young people's parties and similar events. And, on the practical side, each club sees that adequate moorings are provided, and co-operates with the navigation authority and neighbouring clubs on matters of common concern. All clubs have their own burgees; most have ties, blazer, cap and car badges, and brooches.

There is companionship and fun in belonging to a boat club, for husbands, wives and children alike. It's also a good way to improve one's knowledge of boats and waterways (for the members of every club represent a vast accumulation of experience) and is of practical value in ensuring that boating facilities are provided, and in circulating useful information about local conditions. There are too many

136

clubs to list. Some are grouped, like the Trent Boating Association or the Association of Nene River Clubs; most belong to the Royal Yachting Association, 5 Buckingham Gate, London, SW1, who publish a year book of affiliated clubs at 17½p post free. Information may also be obtained from the Association of Waterways Cruising Clubs, Sec: C. Stephens, 38 Sandhurst Drive, Ilford, Essex.

WATERWAY SOCIETIES

There are also the waterway societies, national, regional and local.

At the top of the pyramid are the three national bodies. The *Inland Waterways Association* is mainly propagandist, seeking to restore and extend the inland waterway system by influencing public opinion. It has seven regional branches, organises an annual rally and other national events, and issues a bi-monthly bulletin. The *Inland Waterways Protection Society* is also propagandist. The *Railway & Canal Historical Society* only concerns itself with history; it organises visits, cruises and lectures, and issues a bulletin and journal.

Regionally, there are Inland Waterways Association and Inland Waterways Association of Ireland branches and Railway & Canal Historical Society local groups, which organise canal and river cruises, visits to places of waterway interest, lectures, film shows, and similar activities, and sometimes issue their own magazines.

Locally, there are a number of societies which concern themselves particularly with an area or with one canal or waterway. Many of these lead a very active life. They may organise rallies, cruises and visits to places of interest during the summer, lectures, film and slide shows during the winter, and issue newsletters. In addition most have developed friendly relations with British Waterways or the local navigation authority which enables them to discuss anything wrong with their waterway direct with responsible officers. This in turn leads to volunteer activities to improve the state of appearance of the waterway—clearing rubbish, painting, weed clearing, etc. Volunteer working parties have their own monthly magazine, *Navvies Notebook* (25p pa from editor, Graham Palmer, 4 Wentworth Court, Wentworth Avenue, London, N3). This kind of activity, social as well as useful, leads on to actual canal restoration work. At present this is being extensively done by the *Kennet & Avon Canal Trust* on the waterway between Reading and Bath, and by the *Caldon Canal Society* on the canal branch leading north from Stoke-on-Trent, and elsewhere by others, while the *Staffordshire & Worcestershire Canal Society* recently finished three years of co-operative work with the British Waterways Board to reopen the 16 locks at Wordsley on the Stourbridge Canal. The *Dudley Canal Trust* goes further—it runs public trips through that astonishing tunnel, and intends to restore Park Head locks connecting it to the Dudley Canal.

The Lower Avon Navigation Trust is both a navigation authority and a waterway society, its members having since 1950 reopened the Lower Avon from the Severn at Tewkesbury up to Evesham. The more recently formed *Upper Avon Navigation Trust* is restoring that from Stratford-upon-Avon to join it at Evesham.

You can join any of these that happens to appeal, or any combination, whether or not they are where you live. Most are lively, all throw up companionable, amusing and interesting people who know a great deal about waterways, and many offer practical work at canal improvement, which specially appeals to people with sedentary jobs.

WATERWAY SOCIETIES

General: *Inland Waterways Association,* 114 Regent's Park Road, London, NW1. Gen Sec: R. W. Shopland.
Inland Waterways Protection Society, Sec: Mrs B. Bunker, Gorse-side, Cartledge Lane, Holmesfield, Sheffield, S18 5SB.
Railway & Canal Historical Society, Sec: J. R. Harding, 38 Station Road, Wylde Green, Sutton Coldfield, Warwicks.

Local: *Ashby Canal Preservation Association,* Sec: G. E. Swarbrick, 49 Butt Lane, Hinkley, Leics, LE10 1LB.
Birmingham Canal Navigations Society, Sec: J. B. Phillips, 482 Sutton Road, Walsall.
Broads Society, Sec: Miss P. J. Oakes, 63 Whitehall Road, Norwich, NOR 99F.
Calder Navigation Society, Sec: A. Turner, 33 Moor Lane, Netherton, Huddersfield, HD4 7HF.
Caldon Canal Society, Memb Sec: R. Savage, 1 Cauldon Avenue, Cheddleton, Leek, Staffs, ST13 7EL.
Coventry Canal Society, Sec: A. H. Frearson, 210 Holbrook Lane, Holbrook, Coventry, Warwicks.

Local: *Driffield Navigation Amenities Association*, Sec: A. D. Biggin, The Country Stores, Brandesburton, Driffield, E. Yorkshire.

Dudley Canal Trust, Sec: Mrs J. E. Smallshire, 27 Trejon Road, Cradley Heath, Warley, Worcs.

East Anglian Waterways Association Ltd, Sec: L. A. Edwards, Wych House, St. Ives, Hunts.

Erewash Canal Preservation and Development Association, Sec. R. J. Godwin, Lawn House, Main Street, Etwall, Derby.

Grand Union Canal Society, Sec: R. C. Hampson, Halfway House, Cassio Bridge, Watford, Herts.

Grand Western Canal Preservation Committee, Sec: D. C. Harward, Gotham House, Tiverton, Devon, EX16 6LT.

Grantham Canal Society, Sec: H. W. O. Walker, The Old School House, Knoulton, Nottingham.

Great Ouse Restoration Society, Editor: Donald Cassels, River Cottage, Great Barford, Bedford.

Kennet & Avon Canal Trust Ltd, Sec: D. D. Hutchings, The Coppice, Elm Lane, Lower Earley, Reading, Berks.

Lancaster Canal Trust, Sec: D. Slater, 163 St Albans Road, Lytham St Annes, Lancs.

Linton Lock Supporters Club, Sec: I. B. Close, Rosehurst Cottage, Great Ouseburn, Yorks.

Lower Avon Navigation Trust Ltd, Sec: Ivor M. Beard, Gable End, The Holloway, Pershore, Worcs, WR10 1HW.

Old Union Canals Society, Sec: R. Wild, 61 Knight's End Road, Great Bowden, Market Harborough.

Paddington Waterways Society, Sec: Mrs D. Boyle, 29A Maida Avenue, London, W2.

Peak Forest Canal Society Ltd, Sec: E. Keaveney, 35 Councillor Lane, Cheadle, SK8 2HU.

Pocklington Canal Amenity Society, Sec: Mrs S. M. Nix, 74 Westminster Road, York, YO3 6LY.

Risca Magor & St Mellons Canal Preservation Society, Sec: M. Bevan, 6 Gelli Unig Place, Pontywaun, Crosskeys, Newport, Mon.

Shropshire Union Canal Society, Sec: J. E. Timperlake, 17 Cranmore Avenue, The Wergs, Tettenhall, Wolverhampton.

Local: *Somerset Inland Waterways Society*, Sec: Mrs E. K. G. Sixsmith, Riversleigh, Langport, Somerset.
Southampton Canal Society, Sec: L. Pearce, Ningwood, 4 Somerset Avenue, Southampton.
Staffordshire & Worcestershire Canal Society, Sec: Mrs E. J. Pike, 48 Rushall Manor Road (off Melish Road), Walsall, Staffs.
River Stour Trust, Sec: Mrs P. W. Easton, 182 Temple Grove, Bakers Lane, West Hanningfield, Chelmsford, Essex.
Stratford-upon-Avon Canal Society, Sec: Dr A. G. Johnson, 8 Union Road, Leamington Spa, Warwicks.
Surrey & Hampshire Canal Society, Sec: Miss J. Sparey, 8 Beaufort Road, Maybury Estate, Woking, Surrey.
River Thames Society, Sec: J. Watson Parton, 2 Ruskin Avenue, Kew, Richmond, Surrey.
Upper Avon Navigation Trust Ltd, Sec: J. D. Tompkins, 10 Guild Street, Stratford-upon-Avon, Warwicks.
Worcester/Birmingham Canal Society, Sec: Mrs M. R. Thornett, 'Joseph', Stoke Wharf, Stoke Prior, Bromsgrove, Worcs.

Ireland: *Inland Waterways Association of Ireland,* Sec: Dr Peter Denham, Ashleigh, 2 Vergemount, Clonskeagh, Dublin 6, Republic of Ireland.
River Bann Association, Sec: Dr D. M. Downing, Lisconnan House, Dervock, Co Antrim, Northern Ireland.

(*Note:* These names and addresses may have changed: in case of difficulty, it would be wise to consult the Inland Waterways Association.)

INLAND CRUISING BOOKLETS

These cover most of the navigable rivers and canals of the British Waterways Board which are popular for cruising, and are invaluable. Here is the list:

1 *Cruising on the Llangollen Canal* (Hurleston Locks to Llantisilio). *price* 25p
2 *Cruising on the Trent Waterway* (Shardlow [Wilden Ferry] to Gainsborough). 17p

To Help You Enjoy Your Boat

3 *Cruising on the Lee and Stort Navigations* (Limehouse to Hertford and Bishop's Stortford).   *price* 17p

4 *Cruising on the Staffordshire & Worcestershire Canal* (Autherley Junction to Stourport-on-Severn).   20p

5 *Cruising on the Shropshire Union Canal* (Ellesmere Port to Autherley Junction).   25p

6 *Cruising on the Oxford Canal* (Napton Junction to Oxford).   17p

7 *Cruising on the Fossdyke and Witham Navigations* (Torksey Lock to Boston).   17p

8 *Cruising on the Grand Union Canal*, Part 1 (Regent's Canal Dock and Brentford to Braunston Junction).   25p

9 *Cruising on the Grand Union Canal*, Part 2 (Braunston Junction to Birmingham, and adjoining canals).   25p

10 *Cruising on the Grand Union Canal*, Part 3 (Norton Junction to Trent Lock).   23p

11 *Cruising on the Macclesfield Canal* (Hall Green Junction to Whaley Bridge on the Peak Forest Canal).   17p

12 *Cruising on the Trent & Mersey Canal*, Part 1 (Trent Lock to Great Haywood Junction and associated canals).   17p

13 *Cruising on the Trent & Mersey Canal*, Part 2 (between Preston Brook and Great Haywood including Staffs & Worcs Canal to Autherley Junction).   17p

14 *Cruising on the Severn Waterway* (Stourport to Sharpness Docks, with the Worcester & Birmingham Canal and the Stratford-on-Avon Canal from King's Norton Junction to Kingswood Junction).   25p

15 *Cruising on the Lancaster Canal* (Preston to Tewitfield Locks).   17p

16 *Cruising on the Leeds & Liverpool Canal*   30p

17 *The Stourbridge Canal*. A Cruising Guide.   2½p

All these booklets can be obtained from the British Waterways Board, Melbury House, Melbury Terrace, London, NW1, postage extra. Each is well illustrated with photographs and a detailed plan of the waterway, showing distances, locks and bridges, and the position and distance from the waterway of churches, farms, grocers, garages, letter-boxes, pubs, post offices, railway stations, public telephones and water points. There are also items about places of interest near the water.

Here are some local guides: *The Broads Book*. An excellent guide, with maps, and detailed information (Link House Publications, 37½p); *The Thames Book*. Similar. Also covers the Medway, Lee, Stort, Wey, Regent's and Oxford Canals (Link House Publications, 37½p); *Gateway to the Avon*. Pocket guide with maps and comments, on the river from Tewkesbury to Evesham. From Lower Avon Navigation Trust, 'Gable End', The Holloway, Pershore, Worcs. 25p.

River Wey Navigation & Godalming Navigation (Weybridge to Godalming), 20p; *Birmingham Canal Navigations Guide* (covers canals in the Birmingham Canal Navigations network), 30p; *Caldon Canal Guide*, 25p; *Calder & Hebble Navigation Guide*, 20p; *River Medway* (Allington to Tonbridge), 17½p. These five pocket guides, with maps and comments, are obtainable from Inland Waterways Association, 114 Regent's Park Road, London, NW1.

Kennet & Avon Canal. Brief Guide and History, 12p; *Reading Cruiseway*, 12p. *Bristol Avon Cruiseway*, 12p. These three are available from the Secretary, Kennet & Avon Canal Trust, The Coppice, Elm Lane, Lower Earley, Reading, Berks.

Monmouthshire & Brecon Canal. Illustrated map and guide obtainable from British Waterways Board, Melbury House, Melbury Terrace, London, NW1. 15p.

(*Note:* postage extra in all cases.)

MAPS AND CHARTS

Stanford's *Inland Cruising Map of England for Larger Craft* is included in this book. It is published separately at 50p. Imray, Laurie, Norie & Wilson do a *Map of the Inland Waterways of England* at 53p, which also includes closed canals and river navigations. Shell-Mex & BP do a *Waterway Map—Shell Service for Motor Boats* at 10p, obtainable from Shell and BP garages.

Stanford's do a *Map of the Norfolk Broads and Rivers* at 50p, and one of the *River Thames—Richmond to Lechlade* at 30p. Esso Petroleum do detailed maps of the Thames and the Broads at 5p each, obtainable from Esso garages in these areas. If any difficulty is found in getting them from garages, they will be sent direct from the Advertising Department, Esso Petroleum Co Ltd, Victoria Street, London, SW1, on receipt of a postal order.

15 (*Above*) Fairline 19 de luxe outboard cruiser. See here pottering inland with a small motor, the boat is equally at home offshore with a large outboard. All fibreglass, and available in 2- or 4-berth versions; (*below*) Dawncraft 22 is one of a range of marine ply cruisers specially designed and built for inland cruising. A particular design feature of the outboard versions of these cruisers is that the motor operates through a well for better appearance and extra protection.

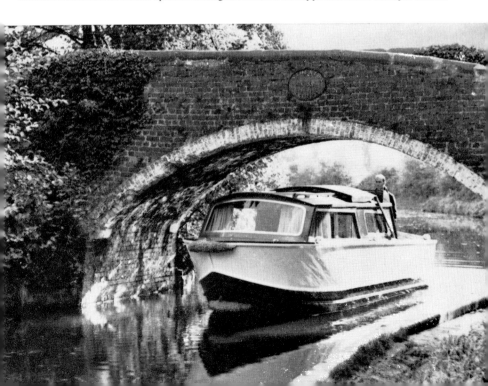

16 (*Above*) 'Winter can be a cruel time for small craft.' Motor cruiser frozen in solidly: note snow-drifts on top of the ice. But careful precautions will ensure small craft take no harm from these conditions; (*below*) happy contrast: a summer boat club rally brings boat owners together for a week-end of cruising, chatting and contests of nautical skill. Often a barbecue, dance or bonfire sing-song rounds off the event.

Others are: *Caledonian Canal Chart*, showing depths of lochs and sea approaches, 25p paper, 37½p stiff covers, post free from Engineer, British Waterways, Clachnaharry, Inverness.

Tidal Waters of the River Trent (Cromwell Lock to Trent Falls), 40p post free; *The Yorkshire Ouse* (Trent Falls to York), 40p post free. These two from Sissons & Son Ltd, 33 Bridge Street, Worksop Notts.

Welcome to East Anglia's Fenland and Waterways, Riverside Boatyard, Ely, Cambs., 12½p.

The Rivers Great Ouse and Cam, 50p; *The Upper Reaches of the Great Ouse*, 15p; *River Wey Navigation*, 43p; *River Nene*, 37p; *Kennet & Avon Waterway* (western section, Avonmouth to Devizes), 77p. These five from Imray, Laurie, Norie & Wilson, Wych House, St Ives, Hunts.

Stratford Canal cruising map, 17½p post free from the Canal Office, Lapworth, Warwickshire.

(*Note*: prices postage extra unless otherwise stated.)

Whatever other maps we carry, however, we don't find it possible to cruise without one-inch Ordnance maps in our locker; they show so much that appears on no other map.

BOOKS

L. T. C. Rolt's *Narrow Boat* (Eyre & Spottiswoode, £1·25) is an account of cruising in a converted narrow boat that has become a classic. John Seymour (*Voyage into England*, (David & Charles, £1·75) and Frederic Doerflinger (*Slow Boat through England*, Wingate, £1·75) have written excellent ones. Read also Roger Pilkington's *Small Boat on the Thames* (Macmillan, £1·50) and Rodney Tibbs' *Fenland River* (Terence Dalton, £1·50) about the Great Ouse.

In the helpful handbook department fall Charles Hadfield's little guide, *Canals and Waterways* (Raleigh Press, 12½p); *The Canals Book* (Link House Pubs, 37½p); Lord St Davids' *Watney Book of Inland Cruising* (Queen Anne Press, 42½p); E. and P. W. Ball's *Holiday Cruising on the Thames* (David & Charles, £2·10) and L. A. Edwards' *Inland Waterways of Great Britain and Ireland* (Imray, Laurie, Norie & Wilson, £2·25). The last named is a standard reference book, and can be found in most public libraries.

If you propose to trail your boat, then *Getting Afloat* is a directory of launching sites on canals, rivers, the Broads and the coast (Link House Publications, 17½p).

Excellent background books are L. T. C. Rolt's *Inland Waterways of England* (Allen & Unwin, £3·50) and the heavily illustrated *Canals and their Architecture*, by Robert Harris (Hugh Evelyn, £4·20). Hugh McKnight's *Canal and River Craft in Pictures* (David & Charles, £2·25) is a pictorial record of the commercial craft which once worked on inland waterways, and L. T. C. Rolt's *Navigable Waterways* (Longmans, £2·25) gives archaeological and engineering background.

For general history, Charles Hadfield's *British Canals* (David & Charles, £2·50, paperback, £1·50) and *The Canal Age* (David & Charles, £2) give an overall picture. Useful regional histories for the cruising man are Charles Hadfield's *The Canals of the East Midlands* and *The Canals of the West Midlands* (David & Charles, each £3), Charles Hadfield and Gordon Biddle's *The Canals of North West England*: 2 vols (David & Charles, £2·50 each) and Charles Hadfield and John Norris's *Waterways to Stratford* (David & Charles, £2·10).

For Ireland, three background books that will add much to your enjoyment are V. T. H. and D. R. Delany's *The Canals of the South of Ireland*; W. A. McCutcheon's *The Canals of the North of Ireland* (David & Charles, £2·50 each) and L. T. C. Rolt's *Green and Silver* (Allen & Unwin, £2·10). The Shannon, Barrow and Grand Canal, the main existing waterways, fall in the Delanys' volume. For general information, see L. A. Edwards's *Inland Waterways of Great Britain and Ireland* (Imray, Laurie, £2·25) and P. J. G. Ransom's *Holiday Cruising in Ireland* (David & Charles, £2·25). For Northern Irish waterways, write to the Northern Ireland Tourist Board, 10 Royal Avenue, Belfast, BT1 1DQ. General information on cruising in the Republic can be obtained from Bord Failte, Baggot Street Bridge, Dublin 2.

You will be enthused for motor-boating on European waterways after reading some of Roger Pilkington's 'Small Boat' series, published by Macmillan. Titles have so far appeared about Germany, Holland, Belgium, Sweden, the Skagerrak, Alsace, Bavaria, France and Southern France, the Meuse, the Moselle, the Lower Rhine and Luxembourg. Prices range from £1·25 to £2·50. A short book on overseas waterways is Charles Hadfield's *Canals of the World* (Blackwell, 50p).

For information about cruising on the Continent and in the United States and Canada, consult the travel agencies of the countries concerned. For cruising in the Netherlands and France, inquire from

To Help You Enjoy Your Boat

World Holidays Afloat (Sales & Charter) Ltd, 23 Old Bond Street, London, W1; or Imray, Laurie, Norie & Wilson, Wych House, St Ives, Hunts, who publish handbooks to these countries' waterways.

The current *Canal Enthusiasts' Handbook* (David & Charles, £1·75) contains a mass of information of interest to those interested in cruising on home or overseas waterways. It is a must.

JOURNALS PUBLISHING INLAND CRUISING ARTICLES

Motor Boat & Yachting	17½p fortnightly
Small Boat & Light Craft	15p monthly
Yachting and Boating Weekly	7½p weekly
Practical Boat Owner	17½p monthly

JOURNALS PUBLISHING OCCASIONAL SUCH ARTICLES

Yachting World	20p monthly
Yachts and Yachting	17½p fortnightly
Yachting Monthly	20p monthly

MUSEUMS

A lot of background information about canals is to be had from a visit to the Waterways Museum at the canal village of Stoke Bruerne near Northampton. An old warehouse has been given over to a fascinating collection of items about the past, while outside, a barge-weighing machine holding a narrow boat has been set up in an old lock chamber. Open daily, including Sundays and Bank Holidays, 10 am–12.30 pm; 2–5 pm; 6–8 pm except during the period of Monday closures (see below). The museum is closed on Christmas Day, Boxing Day, and every Monday from the second Monday in October to the Monday before Good Friday, inclusive. During the period of Monday closures, the museum will close at 5 pm every day. Admission, adults 10p, children 2½p. Car park. Teas available. The museum is on the Grand Union Canal near Blisworth tunnel—if you plan to cruise that way, leave time for a visit.

The Cusworth Hall Industrial Museum outside Doncaster has a canal room. Its curator, John Goodchild, is himself a canal enthusiast, as is Dr David Owen of the Manchester Museum. For other collections, see the article on 'Waterways Museums' in the *Canal Enthusiasts' Handbook*.

147

TRADE ASSOCIATIONS (from whom appropriate literature can be obtained).

Canals and Rivers	Association of Pleasure Craft Operators, The Wharf, Norbury Junction, Stafford.
Broads	Norfolk and Suffolk Broads Yacht Owners Association (booked through Blakes [Norfolk Broads Holidays] Ltd, Wroxham, Norwich NOR 41Z
	Broadland Owners Association (booked through Hoseasons Norfolk Holidays, 252 Oulton Broad, Lowestoft).
	Red Whale Boat Owners Association (booked through R. B. Bradbeer Ltd, 7 Battery Green Road, Lowestoft, Suffolk).
Fenlands	Great Ouse Boatbuilders and Operators Association (inquiries to Riverside Boatyard, Ely, Cambs).
Thames	Thames Hire Cruiser Association, c/o W. Bates & Son, Bridge Wharf, Chertsey, Surrey.

In addition, the British Waterways Board, Melbury House, Melbury Terrace, London, NW1, offers a free list of firms with hire craft on its own waterways (and information about its own hire fleet). The Inland Waterways Association, 114 Regent's Park Road, London, NW1, publishes a helpful *Waterways Holiday Guide* (15p post free) which includes a list of boat hirers in all areas.

AUTHORITIES AND CHARGES

Hired craft. Hire charges normally include the licence fee and lock tolls of the authority upon whose water the hire fleet is based. Should you wish to pass off that authority's water, you may have to pay a small extra charge. Consult the firm.

Owned craft. As charges are altered from time to time, it would be misleading to quote actual rates. Inquire from the appropriate waterway authority, stating the length of the boat. For a list of authorities, see the *Canal Enthusiasts' Handbook.*

148

Acknowledgements

We would like to acknowledge the help we received from Mr T. R. Lawrence and Mr J. Backhouse of the British Waterways Board, Mr H. F. Brooker of Blakes (Norfolk Broads Holidays) Ltd, Mr David Wain (Hon Sec, Association of Pleasure Craft Operators), Geoffrey Dibb Ltd, Mr L. A. Edwards (Secretary, East Anglian Waterways Association), Mr John Groves (Chief Engineer, Blue Line Cruisers Ltd), Mr Charles Hadlow (Curator, Waterways Museum, Stoke Bruerne), Mr L. Hales (Secretary, Soar Boating Club), Imray, Laurie, Norie & Wilson Ltd, and Captain L. Munk (Chairman, Inland Waterways Association), and from members of very many hire craft firms, canal societies and others whom we have consulted.

For the second edition we have been much helped by Mr H. E. Cardy of the British Waterways Board, Mr Robert Shopland of the Inland Waterways Association, Mr L. A. Edwards, Mr Hugh McKnight, and the officials of many canal authorities and societies. We are grateful to them all.

We would also like to thank the following for permission to reproduce illustrations: Morgan Giles Ltd, jacket; Blakes (Norfolk Broads Holidays) Ltd and Fox Photos Ltd, plates 1 (a) and 2 (a); Maidboats Ltd, 1 (b); J. A. Smeed, 2 (b); *Motor Boat and Yachting*, 3 (a); British Waterways Board, 3 (b); British Waterways Board, Waterways Museum, 10 (a); F. Leonard Jackson, 4 (a); L. A. Edwards, 4 (b), 5 (a), 5 (b), 6 (a), 6 (b), 7 (b), 8 (b); Stuart Kinch, 7 (a); Blue Line Cruisers Ltd, 8 (a); Malcolm Thomas (Plastics) Ltd, 9 (a); Mustograph Agency, 9 (b); Wyvern Shipping Co Ltd, 10 (b); Inland Cruising Co Ltd, 11 (a), 11 (b); Shropshire Union Cruisers Ltd, 12 (a); Brooklands Aviation Ltd, 12 (b); Orme & Sons (Boat-builders) Ltd, 13 (a); Creighton Caravans Ltd, 13 (b); John Freeman (Marine) Ltd, 14 (a); Norman Cruisers Ltd, 14 (b); Oundle Marine Ltd, 15 (a); Dawncraft Cruisers, 15 (b); *Coventry Evening Telegraph*, 16 (a); W. French, 16 (b). Fig 8 is based on drawings provided by the British Waterways Board.

149

Index

References to most of the subjects covered in this book will be found under headings: Boats, Canals, Engines and Planning a Cruise

151

Boats, accidents to—*cont*
frost precautions with, 130–5; gas leaks in, 66–7; glassfibre-hulled, 110; going aground, 63–4; hiring, 86–101; insurance—against liability for hire fee, 96, of hire craft, 96–7, of owned craft, 109; layouts of, 92–3; maintenance—seasonal, 124, 127–8, spring refitting, 135, while cruising, 56–7, 93–4, 99, winter lay-up, 128–35; mooring up, 67–70; moorings for, 103, 109; narrow, *see* Narrow Boats; navigation lights at night, 55; overtaking other, 61; passing anglers, 60; passing other, 59–61; past blind corners, 73; past bridge-holes, 73–4; plywood-hulled, 110; reversing, 52; ropes on, care of, 57, 127; sound signals, 60–1; speed, 34, 37, 59–60, 70; steering, 50–2; technical terms, 55; trailing, 70, 102–3, 145; turning, 67, 118; waterway charges for, 41, 70, 109. *See also* Bridges, Engines, Fuel, Gas, Maintenance, Propeller
Bonthron, P. B., author, 17
Books, magazines and maps, useful, 140–2, 145–7
Bord Failte (Eire), 146
Bordesley Junction (Birmingham), 42
Boroughbridge, 47
Bosley locks, 24
Boston, 45
Bradbeer, R. B., Ltd, 148
Bramwith Junction, 42–3, 46
Brandon, 48
Braunston, 17, 27, 42–4, 117
Braunston tunnel, 23
Brecon, 46
Brecon Canal, 46, 142
Brentford, 42
Breydon Water, 28
Bridges, canal, cruising through, 73–4; general, 25; lifting and swing, 74

Bridgewater Canal, 24, 26, 42–3, 45
Bridgewater Dept, Manchester Ship Canal Co, 43, 45
Brinklow, 24
British Waterways Board, cruising inquiries to, 40, 45–6, 141–2, 145, 148; establishment of, 20–1; general, 137–8, 147; organisation, 28–9, 32
Broadland Owners Association, 148
Broads Society, 138
Broads, The, 16, 20–2, 26–8, 30–1, 34, 37–8, 47, 91–2, 142
Brownshill lock, 48
Buoyancy jackets, 56
Bure River, 47
Burwell Lode, 48
Buying a boat, 102–13

Calder & Hebble Navigation, 22, 47, 142
Calder Navigation Society, 138
Caldon branch (Trent & Mersey), 21, 45, 142
Caldon Canal Society, 137–8
Caledonian Canal, 23, 145
Cam River, 48, 145
Cambridge, 15, 48
Canada, waterways in, 23, 49, 146
Canals, administration of, 20–1, 28–9; aqueducts, 24, 74–5; bridges and bridgeholes, 25, 73–4; buildings on, 26–7, 29; charges for cruising on, 41, 70, 109; inclined planes, 23; lifts, 23, 45; locks, 22–3, 37, 76–85; navigable channel of, 58, 63; pubs, 14, 26–7, 31–2; restoration of, 21, 137–8; staff, 28–9, 76–7; towpaths, 25–6; tunnels, 23–4, 75–6; water supplies, 27–8
Canal societies, 138–40
Carlow (Ireland), 48
Carrick-on-Shannon (Ireland), 48
Casting off, to start cruising, 57–8
Castleford, 28
Charges, for hiring a boat, *see* Hiring; for moorings, *see* Moor-

Index

Charges—*cont*
ings; for use of waterways, *see* Waterway charges
Chester, 17, 44
Chesterfield Canal, 26, 45
Children, safety of, while cruising, 56, 59, 75
Chirk aqueduct, 24
Chirk tunnel, 26
Christleton, 17
Coltishall, 47
Commercial craft, on waterways, 20–2, 28–9, 60–1, 114–17
Coothall (Ireland), 48
Coventry Canal, 14, 26, 42–4
Coventry Canal Society, 138
Cowroast (Grand Union Canal), 15
Crick tunnel, 24
Cromwell lock (Trent), 28
Crowland, 45n
Cruises, planning, *see* Planning
Cruising, *see* Boats, Buying, Engines, Hiring, Planning
Cruising Clubs, Association of Waterways, 137
Cusworth Hall Industrial Museum, 147

Dane aqueduct, 24
Dee River, 24, 28
Delany, V. T. H. & D. R., authors, 146
Denver Sluice, 48
Derwent Mouth, 42
Devizes locks, 22
Doerflinger, Frederic, author, 145
Doncaster, 21–2, 147
Driffield Navigation Amenities Association, 139
Dublin, 48
Dudley Canal, 23, 42, 44, 138
Dudley Canal Trust, 24, 138–9
Dudley Port, 41
Dudley tunnel, 24, 44, 138

Earith, 34, 47–8
East Anglian Waterways Association, 48, 139

Eckington, 25
Edwards, L. A., author, 145–6
Ellesmere Canal, *see* Shropshire Union
Ellesmere Port, 26
Ely, 48
Engines, boat, controls, 52, 55; diesel, 93; inboard, 93–4, 110–12; 130–2; inboard-outboard transom drive unit, 112; instruments, 58; maintenance while cruising, 93–4, 99; outboard, 50, 63, 93–4, 110–12, 132–3; seasonal maintenance, 127–8; trouble, detecting, 58–9; winter lay-up, 130–3
Enniskillen (Ireland), 48
Erewash Canal Preservation & Development Association, 139
Erne, Lough (Ireland), 33, 48
Etruria (Stoke-on-Trent), 13
Europe, cruising in, 49, 146–7
Evesham, 44, 138

Farmers Bridge locks, 14, 42–3
Fazeley, 42
Fenland waterways, 16, 20–1, 26–7, 33–4, 37, 44, 47–8, 145
Fenny Stratford, 44
Finance, for buying a boat, 104–6, 109
Fire, precautions against, 66–7, 119
Fossdyke, 16, 45, 141
Fotheringhay, 25, 44
Foulridge tunnel, 24
Foxton, 22–3, 40
Fradley Junction, 14, 26, 42–3
France, waterways in, 23, 49, 86, 146–7
Frost precautions, *see* Boats
Fuel, precautions concerning, 56, 66; supplies, on waterways, 40

Gailey, 44
Gainsborough, 42–3
Gas, bottled, on boats, 66–7, 99, 121, 123
Gas fires on boats, 94
Gas leaks, action to take, 66–7

153

Index

Selby, 47
Selby Canal, 47
Severn River, 16, 20, 25–6, 28–9, 33, 41–2, 44, 76, 138, 141
Seymour, John, author, 145
Shannon Harbour (Ireland), 48
Shannon River (Ireland), 33, 48, 146
Shardlow, 15, 26
Sharpness, 44
Sheffield, 21
Sheffield & South Yorkshire Navigation, 21
Shopping, when cruising, 40, 95
Shropshire Union Canal, 14, 26, 42–4, 141. *See also* Llangollen Canal
Shropshire Union Canal Society, 139
Skipton 15, 47
Somerset Inland Waterways Society, 140
Sonning, 46
Sound signals, 60–1
Southampton Canal Society, 140
Sowerby bridge, 47
Speed, when cruising, 34, 37, 59–60, 70
Staffs & Worcs Canal, 26, 42, 44, 141
Staffs & Worcs Canal Society, 138, 140
Stainforth & Keadby Canal, 42–3, 46
Staircase locks, *see* Locks
Standedge tunnel, 24
Stanley Ferry aqueduct, 24
Steering a boat, 50–2
Stockton (Grand Union Canal), 27
Stockwith, *see* West Stockwith
Stoke Bruerne, 15, 27, 147
Stoke Ferry, 48
Stoke-on-Trent, 13, 20, 137
Stoke Wharf, 44
Stone (Staffs), 13–14, 45
Stoppages, notices of, 40, 98
Stort River, 46, 141–2
Stour, River, Trust, 140

Stourbridge Canal, 21, 23, 42, 44, 138, 141
Stourport, 26, 41–2, 44
Stourton, 42
Stratford-upon-Avon Canal Society, 140
Stratford-upon-Avon, 21, 43, 138
Stratford-upon-Avon Canal, BWB section, 79, 141; National Trust section, 21, 43, 145
Streat, Michael, boat hirer, etc, 20
Stretford Junction, 42–3
Surrey & Hampshire Canal Society, 140
Surveying a boat, before buying, 104
Sutton's Stop (Hawkesbury), 15
Swale Nab, 47
Sweden, waterways in, 23, 146

Tardebigge, 22
Teddington, 31–2, 42
Tempsford Bridge, 47
Tewkesbury, 138
Thames Conservancy, 31, 42–3, 46, 110
Thames Hire Cruiser Association, 32, 148
Thames River, 16, 20, 31–2, 42–3, 46, 76–7, 91–2, 121, 142, 145
Thames, River, Society, 140
Thurlwood lock, 79
Thurne River, 47
Thurston, E. Temple, author, 17
Tibbs, Rodney, author, 145
Tidal waters, cruising in, 28, 30, 40, 43, 45, 47–8
Tonbridge, 46
Towing a boat from the bank, 64–5
Towpaths, 25–6
Trailing a boat, 70, 102–3, 145
Trent Junction, 42–3
Trent & Mersey Canal, and Caldon branch, 13–14, 21, 23–4, 26, 42–3, 45, 79, 141
Trent Power Boat & Ski Club, 70
Trent River, 16, 20, 25–6, 28, 42–3, 45–6, 70, 76, 140, 145

157

Index

Tunnels, cruising through, 75–6; general, 23–4; legging through, 26, 75; paths through and over, 26; when open, 40
Turning a boat, when cruising, 67, 118

United States, waterways in, 49, 146
Upper Avon Navigation Trust, 138, 140
Upper Avon River, 21

Wain, D. B. & G. F., boat hirers, 17–18
Wakefield, 21, 24
Walking permits on towpaths, 25
Wallingford, 46
Waltham Town lock, 46
Warwick, 27
Wash, The, 33
Water supplies, to canals, 27–8
Waterway charges, 41, 70, 109, 148
Waterway societies, 138–40
Waterways Cruising Clubs, Association of, 137
Waterways Museum, 147
Waveney River, 47
Weaver River, 20, 23, 45
Weed, on waterways, 38, 40, 48, 58, 62
Weed hatches, on boats, 62, 111
Welford lock, 44
Welland & Nene River Authority, 44, 79
Welland River, 45n
Welsh Canal, *see* Llangollen Canal

West (Wast) Hill tunnel, 24
West Stockwith, 26
Westall, George, author, 17
Weston Marsh, 45
Wey River, 46, 142, 145
Whaley Bridge, 45
Wherries, 21
Widdington Ings, 47
Wigan, 22, 28, 42–3
Wind, effect of, when cruising, 64, 115
Windermere, 33
Wissey River, 37, 48
Witham River, 45, 141
Wolverhampton, 14, 22
Wolverton aqueduct, 24
Worcester, 15, 41–2
Worcester Bar (Birmingham), 14, 41–2
Worcester/Birmingham Canal Society, 140
Worcester & Birmingham Canal, 22, 24, 41–2, 44, 79, 141
Wordsley locks, 138
World Holidays Afloat (Sales & Charter) Ltd, 147
Wroxham, 47
Wyatt, R. H., hirer, 20

Yare River, 21, 47
Yarmouth, 21, 28, 30–1, 47
York, 15, 47
Yorkshire Ouse River, 21, 26, 28, 47, 145
Yorkshire Ouse Navigation Trustees, 47

158